Winning With The

ENGLISH OPENING

D0779574

GM Andrew Soltis

Revised Third Edition

Chess Digest, Inc.

WINNING WITH THE ENGLISH OPENING

First published 1982
Second revised edition 1987
Third revised edition 1997
This is a 1997 revised and expanded edition
Copyright© 1997 Andrew Soltis

All rights reserved under Pan American and International Copyright conventions.

ISBN 0-87568-170-0

No part of this publication may be reproduced, stored in a retrieval system, or transmitted in any form, or by any means: electronic, electrostatic, magnetic tapes, mechanical photo-copying, recording or otherwise, without prior and current permission from the publisher.

Author: Andrew Soltis
Computer Typesetting: Elaine Smith and Roy Devault
Cover: Elaine Smith
Editors: Ken Smith (F.I.D.E. 2365) and Roy DeVault
Final Preparation and Diagrams: Roy DeVault
Final Proof: Roy DeVault
Publisher: Chess Digest, Inc.®, P.O. Box 535699, Grand Prairie, TX 75033

Send the publisher $3.00 for the new Chess Guide that catalogs every chess book for general sale in the United States. You are given publishers, page counts, notation and critical reviews. Also included in the catalog is a free Chess Improvement course for beginners up through Master level players.

TABLE OF CONTENTS

INTRODUCTION · 6

SECTION I · 1 c4 e5 2 g3 · 12

A · **2...Nc6 3 Bg2** · 14
A1 · 3...g6 4 Nc3 Bg7 5 e4 d6 6 Nge2 · 15
A2 · 3...Nf6 · 24
A3 · 3...f5 · 27

B · **2...Bc5** · 29

C · **2...f5 3 Bg2 Nf6 4 Nc3** · 32
C1 · 4...d6 · 33
C2 · 4...g6 · 37
C3 · 4...c6 · 39

D · **2...d6 3 Bg2 c6 4 Nc3 Be6 5 d3** · 41
D1 · 5...Nf6 · 43
D2 · 5...f5 · 45
D3 · 5...g6 · 46
D4 · 5...Nd7 · 47

E · **2...Nf6 3 Bg2** · 49
E1 · 3...d5 4 c×d5 N×d5 5 Nc3 · 50
E2 · 3...c6 4 d4 e×d4 5 Q×d4 d5
6 c×d5 c×d5 7 Nf3 Nc6
8 Qa4 Be7 9 0-0 0-0 10 Be3 · 66

SECTION II · 1 c4 c5 2 g3 · 78

A · **2...e6 e6 3 b3 d5 4 Bb2 Nf6 5 Bg2 Be7** · 80
6 Nf3 0-0 7 0-0 Nc6 8 e3 b6 9 Nc3 Bb7
10 c×d5 N×d5 11 N×d5
A1 · 11...Q×d5 · 88
A2 · 11...e×d5 · 90

B	2...Nf6 3 Bg2 e6 with b7-b6	92
C	2...Nf6 3 Bg2 d5 4 c×d5 N×d5 5 Nc3	96
C1	5...N×c3	98
C2	5...Nb6	99
C3	5...Nb4	101
C4	5...Nf6	103
C5	5...Nc7	104
D	2...g6 3 Bg2 Bg7 4 e3 (e6)	**111**
D1	4...Nf6	112
D2	4...e5	115
D3	4...Nc6	119

SECTION III	1 c4 Nf6 2g3	**131**
A	2...d5	**133**
B	2...g6 (also 2...d6) 3 Bg2 Bg74 Nc3 0-0 5 e4 d6 6 Nge2	135
B1	6...c6	137
B2	6...c5	138
B3	6...e5	141
C	2...e6 3 Nf3 d5 4 b3 Be7 5 Bg2 0-0 6 0-0	**148**
C1	6...c6	149
C2	6...b6	150
D	2...c6 3 b3 d5 4 Bb2	**155**
D1	4...Bg4	156
D2	4...g6	158
D3	4...Bf5	159

SECTION IV   163

    A   1...e6   164

    B   1...c6   166

    C   1...f5 2 g3 Nf6 3 Bg2 e6 4 Nf3 Be7   167
           5 0-0 0-0 6 d3
           C1   6...d5   170
           C2   6...d6   174

    D   1...b6   176

    E   1...d6 and 1...g6   178

INTRODUCTION

If there is one major opening that has undergone a magical transformation over the last generation, it is the English. As late as the 1970's, the main line given in most books was a dinosaur variation (*1 c4 e5 2 Nc3 Nf6 3 Nf3 Nc6 4 d4!?*) that had virtually disappeared from master and amateur chess.

In place of ideas like that were a new generation of English strategies, many involving slowly emerging plans and quiet development schemes — and some with no pawn exchanges in the first 8 to 14 moves. The old adage about bringing out knights before bishops and the warnings about creating holes in the center were all but forgotten.

The attraction of the English, then as now, stemmed in part from its positional approach. White, it seemed, was beginning his middlegame plan with his first move. Without making any obvious errors, Black could find himself with a lost game because his queenside had been overrun by enemy pieces and pawns. Defenders against 1 c4 began to wonder whether the only good counter was to throw themselves into a kingside attack that might take White's attention away from the center and queenside.

Here's a typical example, which might have been played at any time in the last 25 years.

Alterman-Har-Zvi
Rishon-le-Zion 1995

| **1 c4** | **Nf6** |
| **2 Nc3** | |

As we'll see, our system will almost always involve the fianchettoing of White's f1-bishop, but not always with Nf3. For that reason, you'll be seeing 2 g3 recommended in the pages that follow.

| **2 ...** | **g6** |

The King's Indian formation is a natural way of countering White's hypermodern setup. Black refuses to indicate where he will put his central pawns.

3 g3	Bg7
4 Bg2	0-0
5 Nf3	d6
6 0-0	e5

Finally, he makes a commitment. Had White played 5 e4 and 6 Nge2 as we recommend in Section III, he could counter with f2-f4, creating promising chances on the kingside. But the plan he chooses now is also good. White will expand on the queenside, the area of the board that falls naturally under his sway.

7 d3	Nbd7
8 Rb1!	

This is how White often blows away whatever opposing force Black can muster on the queenside — b2-b4-b5 or in connection with c4-c5. In the short run, Black can gain temporary control of the a-file. But the short run ends at move 14.

8 ...	a5
9 a3	Nh5

Not 9...c5 because 10 b4 a×b4 11 a×b4 c×b4 12 R×b4 exposes the b7-pawn to greater pressure.

10 b4	a×b4
11 a×b4	f5

Understandably Black wants to get his kingside counterplay rolling before he is overwhelmed on the opposite wing. He can take certain liberties in terms of time — but not in terms of caution — in a semi-closed position like this. For these reasons, 11...h6! should have been played.

12 Bg5!

Here's the problem with his last move. Black doesn't want to give away his fianchettoed bishop (*12...Bf6*) and can't afford 12...Qe8 13 Nd5!, threatening the pawn and fork at *c7*. And retreating his h5-knight to *f6* is too embarrassing.

12 ...	Ndf6
13 Qd2	f4

14 Ra1

Now we see the wisdom in opening the a-file. Whether Black exchanges rooks or concedes the a-file immediately, he will have problems when White plays Ra7!.

14 ...	Rb8
15 Ra7	Bg4
16 Qa2!	

Maximizing the pressure on two key lines, the a-file and the a2-g8 diagonal. Note also that White's move clears the way for Nd2, unveiling an attack of the g2-bishop on *b7*.

16 ...	Kh8
17 Nd2	c6

18 Qa5!

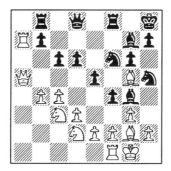

Endgames are often quite good for White in the English. Now 18...Q×a5 19 b×a5! exposes *b7* to even more pressure after Rb1

18 ...   Qc8

No better is 18...b6 since Black's queenside falls apart soon after 19 Qa4

19 b5

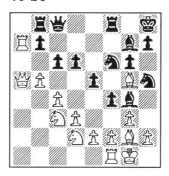

This is the kind of middlegame White had in mind when he nudged his QR one square to the right at move 8.

19 ...   f×g3
20 h×g3   Bh3

(see diagram on next page)

Desperation comes early. Black cannot defend the queenside any more (*20...c5 21 Qb6*).

21 b×c6	B×g2
22 K×g2	Qg4

The endgame that follows 22...b×c6 23 Qc7! was also hopeless.

23 Nde4

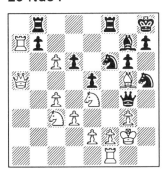

This is another common theme in the English — the occupation of central light-colored squares by his knights. (And not 23 B×f6 Nf4ch 24 Kg1 Qh3 25 g×f4 Qg4ch with a saving perpetual check.)

23 ...	N×e4
24 N×e4	Q×e2
25 R×b7	Rbc8

(see diagram on next page)

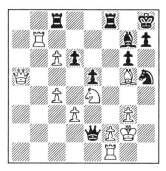

Or 25...Q×d3 26 Qd5 Qf3ch 27 Kg1. When the attack is over, White's c-pawns become decisive.

26 Qd5!	Qf3ch
27 Kh2	Qe2
28 Kg1	Nf4

Again trying for perpetual check.

29 B×f4	e×f4

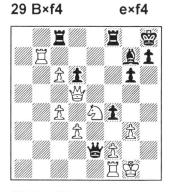

30 N×d6!

Convincing. Black is out of bullets after 30...f×g3 31 Nf7ch R×f7 32 R×f7 g×f2ch 33 R7×f2 Qg4ch 34 Qg2! or the ancient smothered mate after 31...Kg8 32 Nh6ch.

The English is a formidable weapon that is still very much evolving. We've organized in the following pages a relatively simple system of variations built around 1 c4 that should become a solid point-scored for any improving player.

SECTION I

1 c4   e5

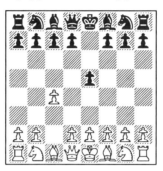

This raises a natural question: "If the Sicilian Defense (*1 e4 c5*) is so good for Black, how can a Sicilian Reversed (*1 c4 e5*) also be good for him?" After all, in the Reversed Sicilian White has an extra tempo-that is one move more than Black usually enjoys and puts to use in a normal Sicilian. Yet the normal Sicilian remains among the most popular of openings at all levels of competitive chess while 1...e5 continues to be the preference of many of the world's best players (including Anatoly Karpov, Boris Spassky, Victor Korchnoi, Mikhail Tal, Bent Larsen, and Vlastimil Hort.

One answer to the question is to understand the different attitudes. With 1 e4 c5 Black is playing <u>to</u> <u>equalize</u> — although he usually equalizes through aggressive counterplay. But after 1 c4 e5 White is playing <u>for</u> <u>advantage</u> in the early part of the game. This difference means, for example, that White will most likely play for d4 in the Sicilian Defense but Black may delay or avoid this provocative line-opening move in the English. White, in the English, may have to open the game up himself.

2 g3

(see diagram on next page)

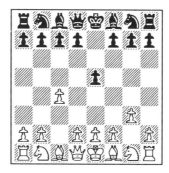

This move, ignored up until recently, has widened the choice of strategies for White and at the same time helps him avoid the most heavily analyzed variations available for Black. Its basic aim is the control of *d5* — the same goal of the more common 2 Nc3. But fianchettoing the Bishop quickly-and delaying the development of the QN-has specific benefits. White's QN remains at home, thereby avoiding the harassment of d5-d4 and the positional complications of ...B-b4×c3. In this latter regard, White doesn't have to concern himself with the currently popular lines such as 2 Nc3 Nf6 3 g3 Bb4 or 3 Nf3 Nc6 4 g3 (or *4 e3*) Bb4.

On the other hand, White commits his Bishop to *g2* with his second and third moves, whereas he could still develop it at *e2* or *d3* if he plays the normal 2 Nc3. But the cases of non-fianchetto development by White in the English are rare, and 2 g3 does not give up any major options.

Let's see how it works. Black has a wide variety of moves, but relatively few independent lines.

They include:

A   2...Nc6
B   2...Bc5
C   2...f5
D   2...d6
E   2...Nf6 (Our main line)

A

(1 c4 e5 2 g3)

2 ...   Nc6

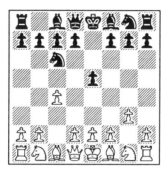

This heads the game toward what might be called a normal Closed Sicilian Reversed, similar to what happens with opposite colors after 1 e4 c5 2 Nc3 Nc6 3 g3. In the diagram Black decides against contesting White's *d5* square but stakes out a claim of his own on the *d4* square. He usually reinforces his control of *d4* with a Bishop, developed at *g7* or, in some rare instances, at *c5*. Black can attack in the middlegame with ...f5-f4 or with d6, Be6, Qd7 and Bh3.

But this will <u>not</u> be a normal Closed Sicilian Reversed because White has played 2 g3 instead of Nc3. This gives him a useful extra tempo with which to contest Black's control of *d4*. He may even occupy that square with his own plan if Black dawdles.

3 Bg2

Now we consider:

      A1   3...g6
      A2   3...Nf6
      A3   3...f5

A1

(1 c4 e5 2 g3 Nc6 3 Bg2)

3 ...   g6

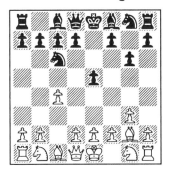

Black's last move is consistent with the Closed Sicilian Re-versed plan and is probably essential to keeping control of at least some of the center. With anything else, Black permits White to seize the high ground with e3 and d4.

4 Nc3   Bg7

White could have achieved e3 and d4 by choosing 4 e3 in-stead of the Knight move. But Black's order of moves — notice he hasn't blocked his Bishop with his KN — has taken the sting out of the d4 plan. In fact, had White played for *d4* he would not be able to maintain that for long because of ...Ne7-f5.

Instead, White finds another center strategy.

5 e4

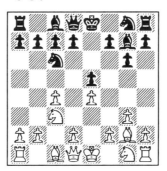

This was a favorite plan of former World Champion Mikhail Botvinnik, and one he used in a number of similar positions. Botvinnik often built up tremendous wing attacks with b2-b4 on the Queenside and f2-f4 on the Kingside. Black must be careful — even though his control of *d4* is secure — because a two-front war is dangerous to the player with less maneuvering space. He must be prepared for example, to meet f2-f4 with his own f7-f5 (or e5×f4 and then f7-f5) in order to stop f4-f5. If he blocks his own f-pawn with a Knight, he can be run over.

This is illustrated by the following: 5...d6 6 Nge2 Nf6?! 7 0-0 0-0 8 f4! and now 8...Nd4 9 d3 c5 10 f5! secures an edge for White. He threatens to advance all his Kingside pawns, particularly g4-g5 followed by f6, and doesn't worry about 10...g×f5 because the open lines that appear after 11 Bg5! give him a powerful game. Black's centralized Knight is impressive but can be exchanged off anytime, e.g., 10...Ne8 11 g4! g5 12 Nd5 f6 13 N×d4 e×d4 14 b4! (Ojanen-Lihflaender, Finland 1955) and White will operate with big threats on the two wings.

5 ...	d6
6 Nge2	

(see diagram on next page)

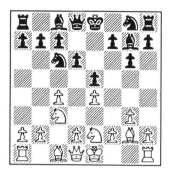

Now we examine two lines:

> **A11** 6...f5
> **A12** 6...Nge7

A11

(1 c4 e5 2 g3 Nc6 3 Bg2 g6 4 Nc3 Bg7 5 e4 d6 6 Nge2)

6 ...   f5

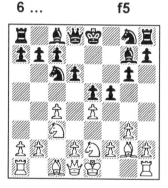

This line is ambitious, intending to build up counterplay immediately on the Kingside. However, a drawback of this move is
that it permits White to open the KB's diagonal after e×f5.
White can also delay the exchange on *f5* since Black only
strengthens the White center if he plays f×e4. Our main line is
based on this second consideration.

7 d3

(see diagram on next page)

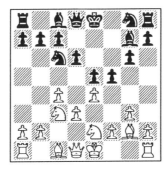

Now Black has two ways to deploy the KN:

A11a   7...Nh6
A11b   7...Nf6

A11a

**(1 c4 e5 2 g3 Nc6 3 Bg2 g6 4 Nc3 Bg7 5 e4 d6 6 Nge2 f5
7 d3)**

7 ...   Nh6

In the last few years Black has tried to refine his play with 7...Nh6, preserving the *e7* square for a possible retreat by the QN and using the KN as an aggressor (at *g4*, or, after an exchange of pawns, at *f5*) or a defender, at *f7*.

8 h4!

The routine 8 0-0 0-0 9 Nd5 g5!? (as in the game Smejkal-Kindermann, Thessaloniki 1984) 10 e×f5 B×f5 11 h3 g4! gives Black active Kingside play — 12 h4 Be6 13 b4 Nf5 14 Be3

Qd7 15 b5 Nd8 followed by ...c6 and ...Nf7. But as a rule of thumb, it is generally dangerous for Black to develop his KN on the rim before White has castled. As Mikhail Botvinnik demonstrated in a famous game (from a slightly different position) White has a strong game by advancing with h4! with the idea of h5×g6.

8 ...	0-0
9 Bg5!	Qd7
10 Nd5	

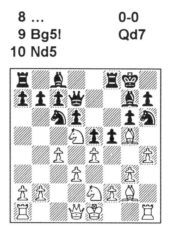

White is clearly better. After 10...Nf7 White should avoid the superficial 11 Bf6? because of the rejoinder 11...Nfd8!. Instead White should simply retreat the Bishop to e3 in preparation for opening the h-file. In the game Chernin-Kupreichik, USSR Championship 1985, Black was on the defensive on both sides of the board after 11 Be3 Ncd8 12 h5 c6 13 h×g6! h×g6 14 Ndc3 Ne6 15 e×f5! g×f5 16 Qd2.

A11b

**(1 c4 e5 2 g3 Nc6 3 Bg2 g6 4 Nc3 Bg7 5 e4 d6 6 Nge2 f5
7 d3)**

7 ...	Nf6

This is more natural than 7...Nh6.

8 0-0	0-0
9 Nd5	Be6
10 Bg5	Qd7

Of course not 10...h6 as after 11 N×f6ch B×f6 12 B×h6 White wins a pawn.

11 Qd2	Rab8

Better is 11...Rf7 and 12...Raf8.

12 Rac1	b6

So that Black can move his QN without allowing the marauding Qa5.

13 b4!

So far as in the game Ljubojevic-Meulders, S.W.I.F.T. 1987, which continued 13...Nd4 14 N×d4 e×d4 15 B×f6! B×f6 16 e×f5. Now 16...g×f5 allows White to gain space with 17 Qf4 c5 18 b×c5 b×c5 19 Rb1. But 16...B×f5 17 N×f6ch R×f6 18 Qf4 was even worse since 18...c5? allows White to win a piece with 19 g4!. A typical example of White's strategy.

A12

(1 c4 e5 2 g3 Nc6 3 Bg2 g6 4 Nc3 Bg7 5 e4 d6 6 Nge2)

6 ...	Nge7

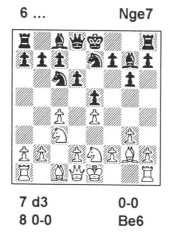

7 d3	0-0
8 0-0	Be6

Black is still too loosened up after 8...f5 by a subsequent exchange of pawns on his f5. White's edge should be clear after 9 Nd5 h6 10 e×f5 g×f5 11 f4 or 10...B×f5 11 h3 and 12 g4 for example.

Since White often gets a good middlegame from e×f5, opening up lines for his g2 Bishop, a good alternative here for Black is 8...Bg4 and then 9 f3 Be6. This leads into our main line with a slight difference in White's extra move — f3.

Although his KB is more pawn-bound than usual, White still stands well if he keeps in mind the plans of queenside (b4-5) and central (d4) expansion. For example, 10 Nd5 f5 11 Be3 Qd7 12 Qd2 Rae8 13 Rae1 prepares the central push. One recent example of this-Sunye Neto-Kindermann, Dubai 1986-went 13...Nc8 14 b3 Nd8 (preparing ...c6) 15 e×f5! and now 15...g×f5 16 f4! is excellent for White as was the game continuation, 15...B×f5 16 d4! Nf7 17 d×e5 N×e5 18 Nd4.

9 Nd5

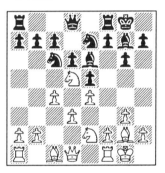

This points up another benefit of the pawn on *c4*. The Knight is superbly posted on *d5* and shields the White center from Black's pieces. This shielding effect may enable White to get in a delayed d3-d4 — which tends to be much more effective than earlier because now Black's pieces have been developed upon the assumption that d3-d4 would never be played. For example, 9...Qd7 10 Be3 Kh8? (The chess version of "I pass") 11 d4! with a clear superiority. One illustration was 11...Ng8 12 N×c7! Q×c7 13 d5 Nd8 14 d×e6 N×e6 15 Rc1 Ne7 16 Qd2 Nc6 17 f4 and White was winning (Uhlmann-Adorjan, Arandelovac 1976).

An improvement is 10...f5 11 Qd2 Rf7 after which White has promising play on the kingside with 12 Rae1 and 13 f4 or on the queenside. An example of the latter is 12 Rac1 Raf8 13 b4 f4!? 14 g×f4 Bh3 15 N×e7ch N×e7 16 f3 B×g2 17 K×g2 e×f4 18 N×f4 c6 with some compensation for Black's pawn (Psakhis-Jansa, Andorra 1994).

Black is better served by 9...f5-our main line here.

9 ...   f5

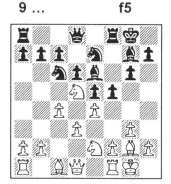

Once again White can play e×f5, followed by h3 or f4 depending on how Black recaptures on *f5*. But White can also ignore the Kingside and center for the time being by expanding on the Queenside. The Russian analyst Shatskes gives 10 Rb1 Qd7 11 b4 as leading to an advantage after either 11...Rae8 12 b5 Nd8 13 Ba3 or 11...Rf7 12 b5 Nd8 13 Bg5!.

The Closed Sicilian Reversed with ...Nc6 doesn't quite equalize. But neither should similar Closed Sicilian Reversed lines with other piece developments.

A2

(1 c4 e5 2 g3 Nc6 3 Bg2)

3 ...   Nf6

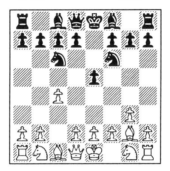

"This move can't be bad, " a player schooled in traditional principles will say. "After all, aren't you supposed to bring out Knights before Bishops?" That principle is grounded in common sense and an underlying theory. The theory is that you shouldn't set your Bishops too early in the game because there is likely to be a shift in pawn structure that will affect them. Knights can easily adjust to such changes, Bishops can't.

But here is a case where Knights are clumsy developers because they permit White to advance aggressively with his pawns.

4 Nc3

White stops Black from his own advance (*4...d5*) and prepares e3/d4.

4 ...   Bc5

(see diagram on next page)

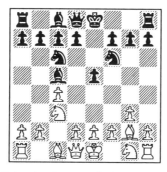

Black might as well try to forestall the e3/d4 advance with this 19th century move.

More in keeping with Black's modern strategies is 4...g6 (instead of *4...Bc5*), but it is already too late. White can engineer d4 again thanks to misplacement of Black's KN-it should be on e7. After 4...g6 5 e3! Bg7 6 Nge2 d6 7 d4 0-0 8 0-0 Bd7 9 h3!, White can follow with a slow buildup of his force in the center (b3, Bb2, Qd2) that will eventually be released by an exchange of pawns in the center. For strategies with 4...Bb4, see the similar position explored in A3. A finesse here is 4...Bb4 and then 5 Nd5 Bc5. The idea is that by provoking the advance of a knight which can be exchanged off, Black is in a somewhat stronger position than after 4...Bc5. For instance, 6 e3 d6 7 Ne2 Bg4 8 h3 Bh5 and now, instead of 9 0-0 N×d5! 10 c×d5 Ne7 as in Hansen-Almasi, Groningen 1995, White does better with 9 d4!, since 9...N×d5 10 c×d5 Bb4ch 11 Kf1! wins material as does 9...e×d4 10 e×d4 N×d4? 11g4!.

5 e3!	0-0
6 Nge2	d6
7 0-0	Re8
8 d4	Bb6
9 h3	

(see diagram on next page)

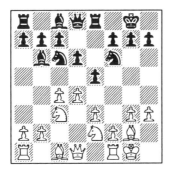

A useful move in this and similar positions. It stops the only move that would effectively add pressure to *d4*, ...Bg4.

9 ...	Bf5
10 d5	Nb8
11 g4!	Bd7
12 Ng3	

So far as in the game Korchnoi-Szabo, Bucharest 1955. White continued with Kh2 and f2-f4 with a crushing attack. Note how despite 10 d5, which should help the scope of Black's bishop, it still "bites on granite" at *e3*. Black's pieces are clearly in retreat and, more significantly, the board has been divided by the center pawns into a sterile Queenside and a potentially explosive Kingside.

A3

(1 c4 e5 2 g3 Nc6 3 Bg2)

3 ...   f5

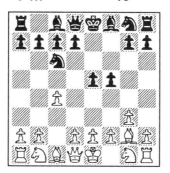

This is similar to a variation of the Sicilian in which White attacks without opening the center with d2-d4 (e.g., *1 e4 c5 2 Nc3 Nc6 3 f4 g6 4 Nf3 Bg7 5 Bc4* and ultimately f4-f5). But the extra tempo that makes the English different from the Sicilian is again significant. Black never gets a chance for a timely f5-f4.

4 Nc3   Nf6
5 e3!

Black faces the unpleasant prospect of that d2-d4 idea once more. If he develops his KB on *c5*, White will kick it back with 6 Nge2 and 7 d4.

5 ...   Bb4

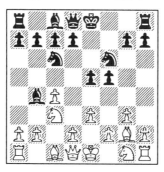

On 5...Be7 all resemblance between the attacking Closed Si-cilian and this conservative opening set-up is broken. White has an easy time of it with 6 d4 and to avoid disadvantage, Black will eventually have to play e5-e4. This brings up an-other theme of the English: Black cannot maintain a pawn chain with units at *e4* and *f5* unless they also have support from another pawn at *d5*. Here, *d5* is unlikely, so White can liquidate the center to his advantage whenever he wants, e.g. 6...e4 7 f3! 0-0 8 Nge2 Bb4 9 0-0 B×c3 10 N×c3 e×f3 11 Q×f3 followed by Bd2, Rae1, and Nd5 (Botvinnik-Simagin, USSR Championship 1952).

6 Nd5!

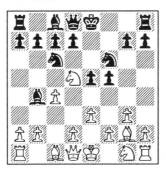

Now 6...N×d5 7 c×d5 gives Black two misplaced pieces (the Bishop on *b4* and the Knight, wherever it ends up) while ena-bling White to attack along the half-open c-file. The doubled d-pawns are not a weakness, but rather a strength: the forward one at White's *d5* will inhibit Black's pieces considerably and Black may be forced to eliminate it by c6-thereby opening up White's fianchetto diagonal.

B

(1 c4 e5 2 g3)

2 ...	Bc5

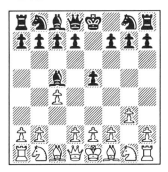

Comparing this with the normal Sicilian (*1 e4 c5 2 Bc4*) we should know that the Bishop development is clumsy because it runs into a wall of enemy center pawns. The only difference is that with the 2 g3 English setup, White may be reluctant to weaken his white-colored squares by combining *g3* and *e3*. As we've seen from Section (A), this isn't a serious concern.

3 Bg2	Nf6

3...Nc6 would transpose into the note to Black's third move in Section (A). The text is aimed at promoting d7-d5 and perhaps Ng4.

4 Nc3	c6
5 e3!	d5

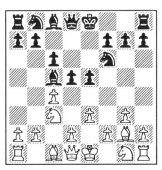

Black's move is the only consistent one, others lead to the kind of positional suffocation cited in the Korchnoi-Szabo game of (A). A similar case is 5...0-0 6 Nge2 Bb6 7 d4 d6 8 0-0 Re8 9 b3 Nbd7 10 Ba3 when White has a fine game — and Black doesn't have a particularly good move. In Olafsson-Keller, Zurich 1959 he tried to regroup with 10...Nf8 and was overwhelmed by 11 d5! which either opens the center or forces the horrible 11...c5.

6 c×d5	c×d5
7 d4	

White must anticipate ...d5-d4, and this move fits in well because he hopes to exchange his d-pawn for Black's e-pawn. Ideally White would like to have his KN already developed so he can recapture on *d4* at move 8 with a Knight, and later expose the isolated Black d-pawn to attack from three pieces. But as it is, White must recapture with a pawn and reach a symmetrical pawn structure. Nevertheless, his superior piece placement puts him on top.

7 ...	e×d4

Of course, 7...Bd6 loses the d-pawn to 8 d×e5 and 9 N×d5.

8 e×d4	Bb4

(see diagram on next page)

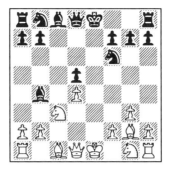

The middlegame will focus on the coming White attack on Black's center pawn with Ne2-f4 and Bg5×f6. The move 8...Bb4 anticipates that by reducing some pressure on the pawn (...B×c3). Clearly 8...Be7 9 Nge2 0-0 10 0-0 Nc6 11 Nf4 or 11 h3 isn't fun for Black to play.

9 Nge2	0-0
10 0-0	h6

Black should try to stop 11 Bg5, which would threaten 11 N×d5 or 11 B×f6 Q×f6 12 N×d5. But it should be obvious that White has a lead in development and an initiative in the center. He has several good moves, 11 Qb3 which threatens the enemy Bishop and center pawn, 11 Nf4 or 11 h3. Black's is not an easy game to play inasmuch as his d-pawn can come under swift assault, while Black has no countervailing pressure on *d4*.

C

(1 c4 e5 2 g3)

2 ...   f5

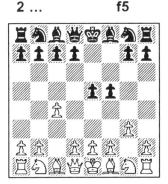

This has independent value only if Black avoids Nc6, which would transpose back into Section (A), or 2...Bc5 which could enter (B).

3 Bg2   Nf6

This is another aggressive formation for Black, similar to the normal Sicilian line which begins 1 e4 c5 2 f4. We know from (A) that e3 and d4 are appropriate responses to f7-f5, but the absence of Nc6 gives Black some greater options. He can play e5-e4 at some point, followed by c6 and d5 to reinforce his center. Then White's KB would "bite on pawn granite". Fortunately, accurate play by White — plus the extra tempo compared with the Sicilian — is enough to handle the Black strategy.

4 Nc3

(see diagram on next page)

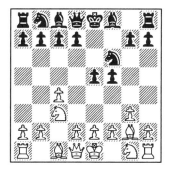

We now examine three Black alternatives:

C1   4...d6
C2   4...g6
C3   4...c6

C1

(1 c4 e5 2 g3 f5 3 Bg2 Nf6 4 Nc3)

4 ...   d6

Now that White brought out his QN, Black has another square for his KB besides *e7*. But 4...Bb4 doesn't seem to fit in well with a pawn on *f5*. For example, 5 Qc2 intending 6 a3 B×c3 7 Q×c3 as well as 6 Q×f5 is a good antidote.

5 e3

Since there is no Black Knight developed on *c6* White is in no rush to play d4, but he would like to bring his KN out to *e2* in order to forestall f5-f4. Black can make that liberating pawn move even as a sacrifice in some cases because his pieces, principally his QB and KN benefit from the advance.   White must watch the *f4* square carefully.

5 ...   Be7

Black could also play 5...c6 and transpose back into the main line after 6 d4 Be7.

6 Nge2   c6

Black can delay a decision about his Queenside pieces and center for a move by castling, but White will also pass by castling himself.   Note that e5-e4 is always premature before White has played d4.   This is because White can liquidate the enemy e-pawn with d2-d3 and the exchange is almost always favorable for White.   (The exchange with e5-e4 and f2-f3 is also promising but not quite as good.) A typical case of this would be 6...e4 7 d3 exd3 8 Q×d3 followed by b3 and Ba3 or Bb2. If Black plays c6, his d6 is very weak. If he avoids ...c6, White will enjoy *d5* for some time as a Knight outpost.

7 d4   0-0

(see diagram on next page)

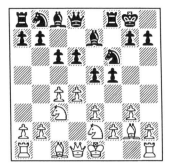

Black doesn't have to worry about the possible ending result-
ing now from d×e5 because his King is not inconvenienced
and his pawns can remain healthy in the center.   In fact,
Black's future in the middlegame may be evaluated entirely in
relation to the center pawns.   If they become fixed on certain
squares-even if they do not come under enemy fire-they will
permit White to seize key outposts.   There will come times, it's
true, in which e5-e4 will be a favorable advance, but Black
must watch this matter with the eye of a jeweler.

White will complete his development by putting his QB at *b2* or
a3.   Black can always close one diagonal with e5-e4 but this
only liberates the other Bishop — and does little for his own
Bishops.   White should be eager to exchange all center
pawns.   For example, 7...Na6 8 b3 Nc7?! could be met by 9
Bb2 0-0 10 c5! with a favorable liquidation (*10...e×d4 11 c×d6!
d×c3 12 d×e7* or *10...d×c5 11 d×e5*).

If Black plays e5-e4 before White exchanges the center
pawns, then White will have to play f3 at some point.   He will
not want to do that immediately if Black can meet f3 with d5.
This is why *7...e4* would be best met by 8 d5!.

(Analysis diagram after 7...e4 8 d5!)

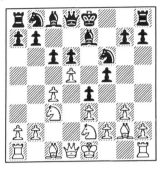

Here White will be able to break the center open with f3, but there is no hurry. He can place his KN on *f4* or *d4* and complete his development now that the center has been arranged to his satisfaction.

8 b3   Nbd7
9 d×e5

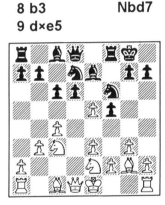

White might be reluctant to exchange here because now Black's QN has a good square on *c5*. But if White plays routinely, say with 9 Bb2, Black is well positioned for 9...e4 e.g., 10 d5 Ne5!.

Black can still put his Knight on *e5* after 9 d×e5 by playing 9...N×e5. But this is not nearly as favorable as in the previous note. White can pile up on the enemy d-pawn with Qd2 and a subsequent Rd1 while bringing his QB to *a3*. Another good strategy is to advance in the center with f4 and e4. Black would have no compensation for a structurally inferior pawn center.

9 ...   d×e5
10 0-0

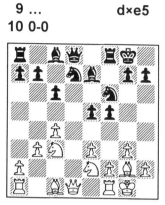

Now White is ready for Qc2, Bb2 and the placing of a Rook on *d1*. He can then open the position with a general Queenside advance (b2-b4-b5) or a well-timed push in the center (e4). On the other hand, Black can use his c5 (and after e5-e4, his e5). But a bit of extra care on White's part should be sufficient to offset any Knight intrusion, e.g., 10...Nc5 11 Ba3 (11...Qa5 12 Na4!) or 10...e4 11 Qc2 Nc5 12 Ba3 intending b3-b4, or 11...Ne5 12 Bb2 Nd3 13 Rad1 and ultimately f2-f3.

C2

(1 c4 e5 2 g3 f5 3 Bg2 Nf6 4 Nc3)

4 ...   g6

Again Black adopts the Closed Sicilian development for his KB. However, White once again can play the annoying e3 followed by d4 strategy.

5 e3	Bg7
6 Nge2	0-0
7 d4	

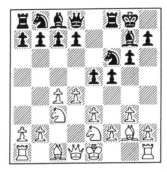

Now if Black advances his e-pawn with 7...e4, then White plays 8 d5 (or 8 0-0 followed by d5) in order to forestall d5 and to open up a diagonal for White's QB, which should be fianchettoed at *b2*. If Black doesn't play e5-e4, White will prepare for d×e5 by b3, Bb2, and Qd2.

Black has yet to declare his intentions in the center (...c6 or ...Nc6; ...d6 or ...e×d4). None of these are particularly dangerous to White. Note that White can even think of Queenside castling (after *7...e4* and a subsequent h2-h4 and Nf4, for instance).

C3

(1 c4 e5 2 g3 f5 3 Bg2 Nf6 4 Nc3)

4 ...   c6

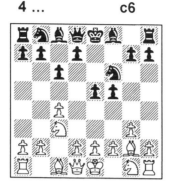

Black seeks to create a massive pawn wall with d5.

This illustrates a point we'll develop further. When Black occupies his *c6* with a pawn he denies his QN its best developing square, and as a result, encourages d4! by White. There is nothing wrong with centralizing your Queen when it cannot be driven back.

5 d4!   e×d4

If Black plays 5...d6 instead, then White has a favorable endgame with 6 d×e5 d×e5 7 Q×d8ch K×d8 8 Bg5 and Queenside castling. Such endgames are not always advantageous, but here the misplacement of Black's King, plus the possibility of assaults on the enemy center (e4) place him in some difficulty.

6 Q×d4!

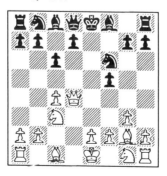

Once Black has played ...c6 White profits from the Q's promi-
nent position on *d4* (no ...Nc6 to drive her away) and from the
backwardness of the enemy d-pawn, since 6...d5 loses a
pawn. Typical play might go 6...d6 7 b3 Be7 8 Bb2 (or 8 Ba3),
0-0 9 Rd1 or even 9 0-0-0!?

D

(1 c4 e5 2 g3)

2 ...   d6

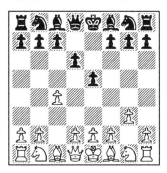

This has limited independent value since a subsequent Nc6 or f5 will likely turn into something we've already investigated. It's actually a kind of waiting move which often seeks a transposition under certain circumstances to a Closed Sicilian Reversed. Similar to this is 2...g6 with the idea of playing Nc6 or f7-f5 later — after White has decided against a e3/e4 plan. Of course, White can still play the Botvinnik policy involving e4/Nge7. He also has another possibility, 3 d4, based on the point that 3...exd4 4 Qxd4 attacks the Rook on *h8*.

For example, 4...Nf6 5 Nc3 Bg7 and now 6 Qe3ch crosses Black up a bit because now 6...Qe7 7 Qxe7ch should favor White a bit, as usual in English endgames. The price of staying in the middlegame, however, is 6...Kf8, after which 7 Bg2 Nc6 8 Nf3 d6 9 0-0 Be6 10 b3 favors White, e.g., 10...Qd7 11 Bb2 Re8 12 Qd2 Bh3 (Mednis-Rotstein, Cannes 1995) and now 13 Nd5! with the ideas of 13...Ne4 14 Bxg7ch Kxg7 15 Qb2ch f6 16 Nxc7! and 13...Nxd5 14 cxd5 Ne5 15 Nxe5 dxe5 (*15...Bxe5? 16 Qh6ch*) 16 Qb4ch and 17 Qxb7.

3 Bg2   c6

If Black refrains from fianchettoing his KB, then 3... Nc6 gets us into new territory. Unlike what we explored in Section (A), Black can then attack quickly with Be6 and Qd7 followed by

0-0-0 and even h7-h5. Even if the attack plan is dropped, Black may benefit from the exchange of White's KB after Bh3.

Since White cannot easily avoid that exchange, he should play 3...Nc6 4 Nc3 and preserve the option of e3/d4. A likely continuation would be 4...Be6 5 Qa4 Qd7 6 e3 Nge7 (Not 6...0-0-0 because White's attack is much faster than Black's after 7 Nb5! Kb8 8 B×c6 or 7...a6 8 B×c6) 7 Nd5.

(Analysis diagram after 6...Nge7 7 Nd5)

English Opening aficionado John Watson gives 7...B×d5 8 c×d5 Nd8 9 Q×d7ch K×d7 10 Ne2 and rates the position as being only slightly better for White. But this kind of position must promise more: Black has no lines for his pieces and may have to play c6, a move that liberates White's KB. No one who plays 1 c4 should be unhappy with this position.

4 Nc3   Be6

Here the natural intention of Black is to play a quiet game in the center without any dramatic advances and simple development of the minor pieces. In the background there lurks the possibility of d6-d5, but White's concentrated power keeps it pretty well hidden.

5 d3

Now Black has four main options:

> **D1**   5...Nf6
> **D2**   5...f5
> **D3**   5...g6
> **D4**   5...Nd7

D1

(1 c4 e5 2 g3 d6 3 Bg2 c6 4 Nc3 Be6 5 d3)

5 ...	Nf6

6 Nf3	Be7
7 0-0	0-0
8 c5!	

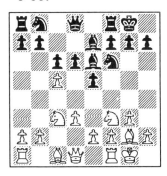

Had Black avoided this game opener (such as with 7...Na6) White would gain a considerable Queenside initiative with 8 Rb1 and b4-b5, a thrust that undermines the Black *c6* square of strength and threatens to open both the c-file and h1-a8 diagonal that so often fall into White's hands in the English.

Here 8...d×c5 9 N×e5 is clearly better for White because of his superior pawn structure. Black must accept the partial dissolution of his center.

8 ...	Nbd7
9 c×d6	B×d6
10 b3	

Now Bb2 followed by Qc2 — and the centralizing maneuver Ng5-e4 — will give White a handsome formation. After 10...h6 we transpose into a game Averbakh-Balashov, USSR 1973 which indicates White's strength: 11 Bb2 Qe7 12 Qc2 Bg4?! 13 h3 B×f3 14 B×f3 Ba3 15 B×a3 Q×a3 16 Rfd1 Rad8 17 b4! Q×b4 18 Rab1 and 19 R×b7.

The problem with 5...Nf6 is that it is development-without-a-plan. Neither the Knight or the Bishop that reaches *e7* have the desired effect on the center.

D2

(1 c4 e5 2 g3 d6 3 Bg2 c6 4 Nc3 Be6 5 d3)

5 ...   f5

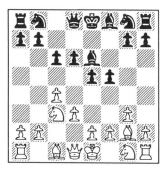

This seems attractive now that White has apparently decided against an e3/d4 thrust in the center. But White can play 6 f4 and 7 Nf3 instead, thereby halting Black's Kingside pretenses (...f5-f4 and g5 are stopped) and pressuring the enemy e-pawn.

If Black plays e5-e4 he surrenders his *d4* to a White Knight and, more seriously, puts a pawn on an indefensible square.

This may all sound negative — White stops this and White stops that. But the secret of playing the English often involves White's ability to anticipate Kingside danger in order to win time for his Queenside initiative. Typical play might run 6 f4 Nd7 7 Nf3 Ngf6 8 0-0 Be7 9 Kh1 h6 (9...0-0 10 Ng5! and the Bishop has no retreat except f7) 10 Nh4 and White threatens Ng6 or f×e5 and N×f5.

D3

(1 c4 e5 2 g3 d6 3 Bg2 c6 4 Nc3 Be6 5 d3)

5 ...	g6

6 e4!

Our friend, Botvinnik's system from Section (A) but with c6 instead of Nc6. The e4 formation effectively stops Black from playing d5 while Black doesn't enjoy the occupation of his *d4* because he can't get a Knight to that outpost after c6.

6 ...	Bg7
7 Nge2	Ne7
8 0-0	0-0
9 b3	

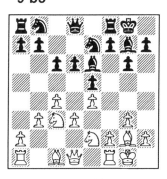

White will follow up with 10 d4 with very good prospects. The presence of a Black pawn on *c6* takes away Nd5 and may prepare ...d6-d5. But it also allows White to be more aggressive in the center.

D4

(1 c4 e5 2 g3 d6 3 Bg2 c6 4 Nc3 Be6 5 d3)

5 ...	Nd7

6 f4!

Thus White assumes an aggressive position in the center. The Black Bishop on *e6* is especially vulnerable now to f4-f5 or Ng5.

6 ...	Ngf6

Black can capture on *f4* of course, but White will retake with a pawn. In fact, if Black is going to make that capture it should be played immediately as 6...e×f4 7 g×f4? allows 7...Qh4ch. But even then he has an unpleasant position following 7 B×f4 Ngf6 8 Nf3 Be7 9 0-0 or 9 Ng5.

7 Nf3	Be7
8 0-0	h6
9 e4	

(see diagram on next page)

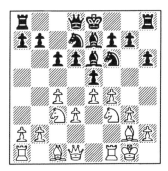

White threatens f4-f5 and thus stands clearly better.

E

(1 c4 e5 2 g3)

2 …   Nf6

This is the most flexible of Black's possible second-move re-plies and also the one most likely to be encountered. It's the most common reply in part because a Black opponent who is uncertain of the differences between White's 2 g3 and the normal 2 Nc3 will probably go along with the move that leaves the greatest chances of transposition into known variations and the least chance of being refuted.

We could have added a separate section on rare second move alternatives, but few are worth a glance.

For example, 2…d5 can be handled easily by 3 c×d5 Q×d5 4 Nf3 and if 4…e4, then 5 Nc3! (e.g. *5…Qf5 6 Qa4ch and 7 Q×e4* or *5…Qc6 6 Ne5 and 7 Qa4ch*).

Novelty is the only virtue to 2…Na6, 2…h5 and 2…Ne7. Each can be met by 3 Nf3 or 3 Bg2 effectively. That leaves 2…c6 to be considered, but it should be considered in its proper space, a few pages from now.

3 Bg2

(see diagram on next page)

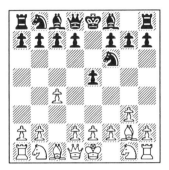

Now 3...Nc6 should look familiar. We met it in Section (A) by way of the move order 2...Nc6 and 3...Nf6. It is still bad (*4 Nc3 Bb4 5 Nd5; 4...Bc5 5 e3*).

After 3 Bg2, Black has two main alternatives:

    E1   3...d5
    E2   3...c6

The first seeks to liquidate his d-pawn and profit from the availability of unoccupied squares at *d5* and *d4*. The latter tries to dominate the center, both the *e5* and *d5* squares, with pawns.

E1

(1 c4 e5 2 g3 Nf6 3 Bg2)

3 ...   d5

This immediate opening of the center is a serious alternative, leading to a Sicilian Dragon Reversed.

4 c×d5   N×d5
5 Nc3

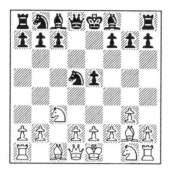

Now White obtains a slight initiative that he should hold for many moves. Black has several possibilities here:

E11   5...N×c3
E12   5...c6
E13   5...Ne7
E14   5...Be6
E15   5...Nb6

E11

(1 c4 e5 2 g3 Nf6 3 Bg2 d5 4 c×d5 N×d5 5 Nc3)

5 ...   N×c3

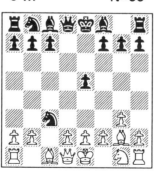

6 b×c3   Nc6

If 6...c5 then 7 Rb1 followed by d3 and the maneuver Nf3-d2-c4.

7 d3	Be7

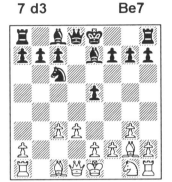

Or if 7...Bc5 then 8 Nf3 0-0 (*8...e4 9 Ng5*) 9 0-0 Bg4 (*9...Be6 10 Ng5*) 10 Rb1 and 11 Qa4 with a plus for White.

8 Rb1	0-0
9 Nf3	Rb8
10 0-0	Be6
11 Qa4	

White has good Queenside pressure. He may continue with Nd2-c4 and threaten B×c6. Note how the pawn on *c3* takes away the Black outpost at *d4*. White can even try for Rd1 and d3-d4.

E12

(1 c4 e5 2 g3 Nf6 3 Bg2 d5 4 c×d5 N×d5 5 Nc3)

5 ... **c6**

Solid but too passive.

6 Nf3

A key move, pointing out the vulnerability of Black's e-pawn. (There's no ...Nc6 now).

6 ... **Qc7**

On 6...f6 7 0-0 followed by 8 d4! is good for White.

7 d4 **e×d4**
8 N×d5!

A good positional move designed to weaken Black's pawn structure.

8 ... **Qa5ch**

9 Nd2	c×d5
10 0-0	Be6
11 Nb3	

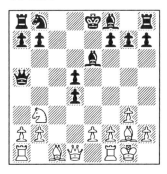

White will follow with 12 N×d4 with a positional edge. Black not only gets stuck defending his isolated d-pawn in this variation; he also loses time with his Queen in doing so.

E13

(1 c4 e5 2 g3 Nf6 3 Bg2 d5 4 c×d5 N×d5 5 Nc3)

5 ...	Ne7

Hoping to focus the Knight on *d4* at some point (Ne7-f5-d4).

6 Nf3	Nbc6
7 0-0	

Now White will advance rapidly with b2-b4.

7 ...   Nf5

White also gets the better game after 7...g6, e.g., 8 b4! Bg7 (8...N×b4 9 Qa4ch and 10 N×e5) 9 b5 Nd4 10 a4 0-0 11 Ba3 Re8 12 Ng5! and the Knight maneuvers to *c5* via *e4*.

8 b4!   a6

Again Black can't take the b-pawn — 8...B×b4 9 N×e5! N×e5 10 Qa4ch.

9 Rb1   Be7
10 a4

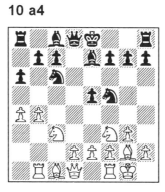

White follows with b4-b5 and occupying *d5* with his Knight with excellent Queenside pressure.

E14

(1 c4 e5 2 g3 Nf6 3 Bg2 d5 4 c×d5 N×d5 5 Nc3)

5 ...	Be6

A natural move, but White still obtains an initiative with accurate play.

6 Nf3	Nc6
7 0-0	Be7

On 7...Bc5 8 N×e5 N×e5 9 d4 favors White's superior development. And 7...Nb6! transposes into the next section.

8 d4!	e×d4

Or 8...N×c3 9 b×c3 e4 10 Ne1! f5 11 Nc2 and White breaks with f2-f3 or advances with Ne3 and d4-d5/c3-c4.

9 N×d4	N×c3
10 b×c3	N×d4
11 c×d4	c6

12 Qa4

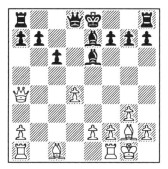

White will follow up with placing Rooks at *b1* and *d1* with fine chances. This illustrates the tactical difference (that makes a strategic difference) between this variation of the English and the comparable line in the Dragon Sicilian. In the Dragon position Black cannot achieve ...d7-d5 because he is a move behind White in our line and must accept the less active alternative of ...d7-d6.

E15

(1 c4 e5 2 g3 Nf6 3 Bg2 d5 4 c×d5 N×d5 5 Nc3)

5 ...   Nb6

This is considered the most crucial line; Black plays 5...Nb6 primarily to help prevent a White d2-d4.

6 Nf3   Nc6
7 d3   Be7

8 a3

Black must decide upon an answer to White's Queenside plan of b4-b5 and Bb2. The choice includes stopping the advance with 8...a5 or strengthening the position in the center with 8...Be6.

E15a 8...Be6
E15b 8...a5

E15a

(1 c4 e5 2 g3 Nf6 3 Bg2 d5 4 c×d5 N×d5 5 Nc3 Nb6 6 Nf3 Nc6 7 d3 Be7 8 a3)

8 ...   Be6

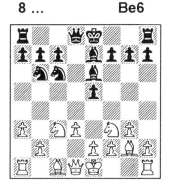

Black intends to develop and castle. If Black had tried 7...Be6 (Instead of *7...Be7*) then White can proceed with 8 a3 f6 9 b4 a5? (This only helps White along by weakening the Queen-side) 10 b5 Nd4 11 N×d4 e×d4 12 Ne4 a4 13 Bd2 Be7 14 Qc1

Bd5 15 0-0 0-0 16 Rb1 with advantage as in Furman-Korchnoi, USSR 1964.

9 0-0

Now we examine three possibilities:

E15a1 9...Qd7
E15a2 9...f5
E15a3 9...0-0

E15a1

(1 c4 e5 2 g3 Nf6 3 Bg2 d5 4 c×d5 N×d5 5 Nc3 Nb6 6 Nf3 Nc6 7 d3 Be7 8 a3 Be6 9 0-0)

9 ...   Qd7

One advantage to this move is the possibility of Queenside castling.

10 b4   a6
11 Ne4!   Bh3

On 11...f5 simply 12 Nc5, while if 11...0-0-0 then 12 Bb2 f6 13 Rc1 and 14 Nc5.

12 Nc5   B×c5
13 B×h3   Q×h3

On 13...B×f2ch White has 14 Kg2!.

14 b×c5   Nd7

If 14...Nd5 then 15 Qb3 0-0-0 16 Rb1.

15 Be3

White retains a strong initiative with the threat 16 Qb3 Rb8 17 Q×f7ch! K×f7 18 Ng5ch.

E15a2

(1 c4 e5 2 g3 Nf6 3 Bg2 d5 4 c×d5 N×d5 5 Nc3 Nb6 6 Nf3 Nc6 7 d3 Be7 8 a3 Be6 9 0-0)

9 ...   f5

Gaining more control of the center (*e4*) and the Kingside, but weakening the e-pawn slightly as f7-f6 is no longer available.

10 b4   a6

After 10...Bf6 White plays 11 e4!, establishing Black's e-pawn as a target — 11...0-0 12 e×f5 B×f5 13 Qb3ch Kh8 14 Ne4 followed by Bb2 and the placement of Rooks on open files.

11 Bb2

White's plan is to exploit the Queenside with an eventual Nc5.

11 ...   0-0
12 Nd2

White will follow up with Nb3-c5 or 12 Na4 with the better prospects.

E15a3

(1 c4 e5 2 g3 Nf6 3 Bg2 d5 4 c×d5 N×d5 5 Nc3 Nb6 6 Nf3 Nc6 7 d3 Be7 8 a3 Be6 9 0-0)

9 ...   0-0

The natural move, leaving various options.

10 b4

White advances on the queenside with one eye on the e-pawn. If Black now pushes the f-pawn two squares he gives up any chance of protecting the brother pawn on *e5*, e.g., 10...f5 11 Bb2 Bd6 12 Rc1 Qe7 13 Na4! with an exchange sacrifice threatened on *c6*. This occurred in Hansen-Hector, Reykjavik 1995, which was clearly favorable for White after 13...N×a4 14 Q×a4 a6 15 R×c6! b×c6 16 N×e5 f4 17 Q×c6.

10 ...   f6

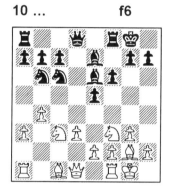

White's dual threats of b4-b5 and Ne4-c5 are so ominous that Black can lessen the impact of one-but not both.

Black can opt for 10...Nd4 (Instead of *10...f6*) taking aim at b3. Then on 11 Rb1 Black can play 11...Nd5 12 Bb2 N×c3 13 B×c3 to eliminate that obnoxious Knight. Here Sunye Neto-Timman, Amsterdam 1985 went into Black's favor with 13...f6 14 e3? Nb5 15 Bb2 c6 16 a4 Nc7 17 Bc3 Qd7 18 Qc2? Nd5 and 19...Rfd8. Much better for White is 14 Nd2! and 15 B×d4 or the immediate 14 B×d4.

Lately Black has been playing 10...Nd4 11 Rb1 f6. White probably does best to avoid a capture on *d4* immediately and play 12 Be3 instead. For example, 12 Be3 c5 13 Ne4 N×f3ch 14 B×f3 c×b4 15 a×b4 Nd5 16 Bd2 and now 16...b6? 17 Qa4 Qe8 18 b5! favored White solidly in Kharitonov-Aseev, Lvov 1990, but 16...Qd7! 17 Qc2 Rac8 18 Qb2 b6 was fairly even in Serper-Assev, Krumbach 1991.

11 Bb2   Qd7

Or 11...Qe8 12 Rc1 Qf7 13 Ne4 followed by Nfd2 and Nc5.

12 Ne4   Rfd8

(see diagram on next page)

On 12...Rad8 13 Qc2 and 14 Nc5 is the right prescription, while if 12...a6 White continues 13 Nc5 or with the subtle 13 Qc2 Bh3 14 Nc5 B×c5 15 B×h3! Q×h3 (Not *15...B×f2ch?? 16 Kg2!*) 16 Qb3ch, after which White can recapture effectively with a pawn on *c5* (*16...Kh8 17 b×c5 Nd7 18 d4!*, Miles-Timman, Tilburg 1984).

13 Qc2

White wants to capture on *c5* with a piece.

13 ...	Bf8
14 Rac1	Qf7
15 b5	Na5

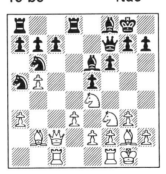

So far as in Portisch-Petrosian, Miksic 1983, which continued 16 Nfd2! (safeguarding *b3* while threatening to breakthrough on *c7*) 16...Nb3 17 N×b3 B×b3 18 Q×c7 Na4 19 Q×f7ch B×f7 20 Ba1 and Bh3! with advantage.

E15b

(1 c4 e5 2 g3 Nf6 3 Bg2 d5 4 c×d5 N×d5 5 Nc3 Nb6 6 Nf3 Nc6 7 d3 Be7 8 a3)

8 ...   a5

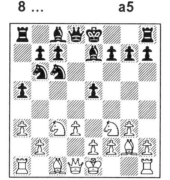

Black plays to restrain White's Queenside expansion via b2-b4. Now White will prepare an alternative strategy-the attack along the c-file with Be3, Rc1, Na4.

9 0-0   0-0
10 Be3   Be6

A fashionable recent move is 10...Bg4.

(Analysis diagram after 10...Bg4)

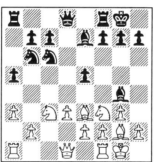

One point of this is the option of meeting Na4 at some point with N×a4 followed by Qd7/Rfd8/B×f3 and ...Nd4. Probably the best sequence for White is an immediate 11 Na4, but 11 Rc1 is also good, e.g., 11 Rc1 Qd7 12 Na4 Nd5 13 Bc5 as above or 12...N×a4 13 Q×a4 Nd4?! 14 Q×d7 N×e2ch 15 Kh1 B×d7 16 Rce1 or 16 R×c7.

Yet another strategy is to capture on *b6* with White's Bishop. For example, 11 Rc1 Re8 12 Nd2!? Qd7 13 Re1 Ra6 14 B×b6! and now 14...R×b6? 15 Nc4! attacks a rook and the e-pawn while 14...c×b6 15 Qa4 allows White to dominate the light squares, e.g. 15...Bg5 16 e3 h5 17 Qb5! and Nd5 or Nce4, and 17 Nde4 as in Petrosian-Psakhis, Soviet Championship 1983. White must not be too concerned in this variation about giving up his dark-squared bishop.

The weakness on Black's *b6* and *b5* because of 8...a5 becomes apparent in all of these lines.

11 Na4

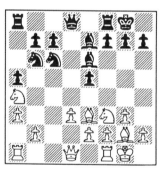

White can also try 11 Rc1 here. In contrast with the 10...Bg4 11 Rc1 positions, White is then preparing d3-d4. An example of that is 10...Be6 11 Rc1 Qd7 12 d4 e×d4 13 N×d4 N×d4 14 Q×d4 Q×d4 15 B×d4 and now 15...c5 16 Be3 Nc4 17 Na4 is very double-edged (Seirawan-Zsu. Polgar, Monaco 1993).

11 ...   N×a4

On 11...Nd5 12 Bc5 White achieves his strategical aim. He can push Black back in the center with a timely e4 and d4. Nonetheless, after 11...N×a4 White "mines" the half-open c-file.

12 Q×a4	Bd5
13 Rfc1	Re8

14 Rc2   Bf8
15 Rac1   Nb8?!
16 R×c7   Bc6
17 R1×c6!   b×c6
18 R×f7!!

The stunning point. So far as in the famous Botvinnik-Por-
tisch, Monte Carlo 1968, which continued in brilliant style with
18...h6 (On *18...K×f7 19 Qc4ch Kg6 20 Qg4ch* followed by
Ng5ch is decisive.) 19 Rb7 Qc8 20 Qc4ch Kh8 21 Nh4! Q×b7
22 Ng6ch Kh7 23 Be4 Bd6 24 N×e5ch g6 25 B×g6ch Kg7 26
B×h6ch and Black Resigned as 26...K×h6 27 Qh4ch leads to
mate.

E2

(1 c4 e5 2 g3 Nf6 3 Bg2)

3 ...   c6

4 d4!

The point of this shot is to saddle Black with an isolated d-pawn and exploit the squares *d4* and *e5* with his minor pieces. It is effective because 3...c6 denies Black the opportunity to hit back at the White Queen when it recaptures on *d4* (*4...e×d4 5 Q×d4* and now *5...Nc6* is impossible).

This should be compared with the slightly different situation arising out of 1 c4 e5 2 g3 c6 which we mentioned earlier. An effective plan for White would then be 3 Bg2 d5 4 c×d5 c×d5 and now 5 d4!. Black's *c6* is now clear so that after 5...e×d4 White would play 6 Nf3 and 7 N×d4 (rather than *6 Q×d4 Nf6* and *7...Nc6* - a position that arises in our main line).

In fact, Black should play 5...e4, but this concedes some key squares such as *f4*. For example, 6 f3 f5 (else the center phalanx collapses following Nc3) 7 Nh3! Nc6 8 0-0 Be7 9 Nc3 Nf6 10 Bg5 Be6 11 Nf4 Bf7 12 e3 and White has a comfortable position. In Seirawan-Miles, Lone Pine 1979, Black castled and found he was already in trouble after 13 f×e4 because neither pawn recapture was safe: (*13...f×e4 14 Bh3! Qd6 15 Nb5* followed by *16 Nc7* or *16 Ne6*) or (*13...d×e4 14 Bh3 g6 15 g4! f×g4 16 B×f6*).

4 ...   e×d4

Recently Black has been trying 4...Bb4ch 5 Bd2 B×d2ch and then ...d6, so that he isn't saddled with a bishop locked inside his pawn structure. But White need do nothing himself in the center and can concentrate instead on the wings. For example, 6 Q×d2 d6 7 Nc3 Qe7 8 e3 0-0 9 Nge2 and White has a choice between expanding on the kingside (h2-h3, g3-g4 and Ng3) or the queenside.

An illustration of the latter is 9...Na6 10 0-0 Re8 11 a3 Nc7 12 b4 Be6 13 b5! and now 13...c×b5 14 c×b5 Rab8 15 d5 Bd7 16 a4 or 13...B×c4 14 b×c6 b5 15 e4 with advantage (Chiburdanidze-P. Cramling, Tilburg 1994).

This falls in with White's plan, but it is not easy to maintain the integrity of Black's pawns in any case. The endgame with 4...d6 5 d×e5 d×e5 6 Q×d8ch K×d8 7 Nf3 and Ng5 may be solid enough for Black to achieve a draw, but it is no fun to play. White has a number of plans in that Queenless position, most involving Queenside castling and f2-f4. Also, White has the attractive alternative of 5 Nc3 Be7 6 Nf3 since 6...e4 allows the typically powerful reassertion of the Knight of Ng1-h3-f4! For instance, Suba-Tseshkovsky, Sochi 1983 went 7 Ng1! d5 8 Bg5 Nbd7 9 c×d5! (more effective now that ...Nc6 has been ruled out) 9...c×d5 10 Qb3 0-0 11 Nh3 Qa5 12 a3 Nb6 13 Nf4 h6 14 B×f6 B×f6 15 e3 Rd8. And now with Black's d-pawn secure, White pointed out with 16 Qc2!! that the enemy Queen had self-trapped itself. To stop 17 b4 Qa6 18 Bf1 Black ended up playing 16...Be7 17 Ra2! Bg4 18 b4 B×b4 19 a×b4 Q×b4, but his position was already lost.

On the other hand, if Black avoids pawn exchanges with 4...e4 - as in the Seirawan-Miles game - White can again play f3 to undermine the enemy center. Or he can play 5 d5! stopping Black from reinforcing the e-pawn with d5. After 5...c×d5 6 c×d5 Bb4ch 7 Nc3, for example, White has a very nice game if Black plays 7...d6?? 8 Qa4ch or 7...Qa5 8 Bd2 N×d5? *(8...B×c3 9 B×c3)* 9 N×d5. Black's best is 7...0-0 but 8 Nh3 leaves White with very pleasing prospects.

5 Q×d4   d5

If Black doesn't advance the d-pawn two squares now, he will be confined to a one square advance later (5*...Be7 6 Nc3 or 6 e4*). The Black pawn is going to be a problem wherever it is and on *d6* it will be harassed by a White Rook from his *d1* and a Bishop at *f4* or *a3*, while being defended by only a Queen and Bishop. On *d5* the Black pawn can be defended more easily — and more important — may advance to *d4* where it tends to be even safer and more aggressive.

6 c×d5

White shouldn't give his opponent a chance to capture on his c4. After 6 c×d5 Black must avoid 6...N×d5 because then he would face problems in moving his KB: 6...N×d5 7 Nf3 Be7? 8 Q×g7.

If Black seeks refuge in the endgame with 7...Nb4 in the above line, then 8 Q×d8ch K×d8 9 Na3 gives him an edge once he posts his QB on the b2-e5 diagonal. For instance, 9...Be7 10 0-0 Be6 doesn't really threaten White's a-pawn because of 11 Bd2! after which 11...N×a2? 12 Nd4 threatens N×e6 and R×a2. Better is 11...a5, but then 12 Bc3 f6 13 b3 c5 14 Nd2! Nb8c6 15 Ndc4 and 16 Nb5 assure White an enduring edge (Cebalo-Miles, Biel 1986).

6 ...   c×d5
7 Nf3

This is similar to — but not the same as — a variation of this opening that is usually reached by way of 1 c4 e5 2 Nc3 Nf6 3 g3 c6 4 d4 e×d4 5 Q×d4 d5 6 c×d5 c×d5. The difference is that White has used his moves to develop his Kingside pieces and also to avoid the impact of Nc6 and d5-d4. The vulnerability of the White Knight on *c3* to d5-d4 is of major significance in that other variation. Here, with the QN still at home at *b1*, it is a different story.

7 ...   Nc6

It is not essential that this move be played, but there is no reason to delay. White's Queen is headed for *a4* when it is hit by the Knight.

8 Qa4   Be7

(see diagram on next page)

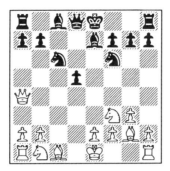

Since White hopes to occupy *d4* with pieces, especially by his Knights, he is not averse to exchanging Bishops with 8...Bb4ch 9 Bd2. Black can try the finesse of 8...Bb4ch 9 Bd2 Be7 in order to deny White the *d2* square for a later Knight shift (Nd2-b3). This leads to sharp play after 10 Nc3 0-0 11 Be3 Ng4!? after which White cannot allow the d-pawn to advance and must try 12 Bd4 N×d4 13 N×d4 Bc5! 14 0-0 (not *14 N×d5 Bd7! 15 Qd1 Be6 16 e4 N×f2!*)

The position is unclear because Black's counterplay on the dark squares may compensate for his weak d-pawn. In Dohoian-Chekhov, Kharkov 1985 White got the upper hand after 14...Bd7 15 Qd1 Qb6? (*15...Qf6!*) 16 N×d5 Q×b2 17 Nb3 Ba4 18 e3! Ne5 19 Qh5.

Black might also play 8...Bd7 here, but there is no real threat (*9...Nb4 10 Qb3*) so White can continue with 9 Nc3 or even 9 Bg5.

A more pertinent alternative is 8...Bc5, seeking a more active square for his Bishop and contesting the *d4* square. Then 9 0-0 0-0 10 Bg5 is the natural way to take advantage of the Bishop's absence from *e7*, with play such as 10...h6 11 B×f6 Q×f6 12 Nc3 d4 (or *12...Be6 13 Ne1* with Nd3-f4 and Rad1 coming up, e.g., *13...Rad8 14 Nd3 Bd4 15 Rac1 Rfe8 16 Nf4* as in Seirawan-I.Sokolov, Wijk aan Zee 1995) 13 Nd5! Qd8 14 Nd2 and Rac1 or 10...Be6 11 Nc3 Qe7 12 e4! or 10...Re8 11 e3 h6 12 B×f6 and 13 Nc3 and Rad1 — Larsen-Chandler, London 1986.

9 0-0 0-0
10 Be3!

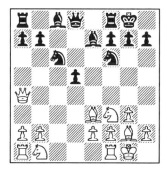

This is relatively unexplored territory, but the early investigation has come back with glowing reports about White's position. His plan is to occupy the dark colored squares such as *d4* and *c5* with minor pieces and attack the d-pawn along the file. Ulf Andersson of Sweden has demonstrated in similar positions how this can be achieved with 8 Qd1 instead of 8 Qa4, but the diagrammed position is much more enterprising. Note that the delay in moving White's QN permits Nd2-b3 as well as Nc3.

We now examine three Black replies at this critical juncture:

E21 10...Ne4
E22 10...Bd7
E23 10...Re8

E21

**(1 c4 e5 2 g3 Nf6 3 Bg2 c6 4 d4 e×d4 5 Q×d4 d5 6 c×d5
c×d5 7 Nf3 Nc6 8 Qa4 Be7 9 0-0 0-0 10 Be3)**

10 ...	Ne4

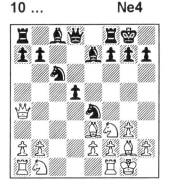

Anticipating Nc3.

The more tempting knight-move, 10...Ng4, should be met by
11 Bd4!, because 11...N×d4 12 N×d4 favors White's centralized pieces and his ability to attack *d5* now that the f6-knight is
gone.

For example, 12...Qb6 13 Nc3 Qh6 and now 14 h3 is good
enough for an edge, but 14 h4 g5 15 N×d5 Bd8 (Suba-Milos,
Spain 1992) requires White to play 16 Nf3! to kill the attack,
e.g., 16...g×h4 17 N×h4 B×h4 18 g×h4 Q×h4 and now 19 Qf4.

11 Nc3!	N×c3
12 b×c3	Qa5

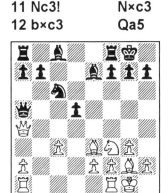

A new idea here is 12...Na5 but it leads to a clear White edge after 13 Ne5! Bf6 14 Rad1 Be6 15 Nd3 — or 13...Be6 14 Rad1 Bf6 15 Nd3. White is ready to kill the d5-pawn with 16 Nf4. After 15...Nc4 16 Bd4 b6 17 Qb3 B×d4 18 c×d4 Rc8 19 Nf4 White stands excellently (Serper-Lutz, Dortmund 1993).

13 Qb3!

White has good play on the two half-open files.

13 ...	Rd8
14 Rfd1	Qa6

To free the QB from defense of the b-pawn.

15 Nd4!	N×d4

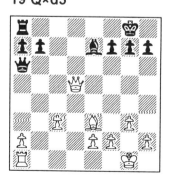

15...Na5 is met by 16 Qb5! Q×b5 17 N×b5 winning material.

16 R×d4!	Be6
17 B×d5	B×d5
18 R×d5	R×d5
19 Q×d5	

So far as in the game Csom-Suba, Kecskemet 1979 which continued 19...Rd8 20 Qb3 Bf6 21 Re1 b6 22 c4 and White won with his healthy extra pawn.

E22

(1 c4 e5 2 g3 Nf6 3 Bg2 c6 4 d4 e×d4 5 Q×d4 d5 6 c×d5 c×d5 7 Nf3 Nc6 8 Qa4 Be7 9 0-0 0-0 10 Be3)

10 ...   Bd7

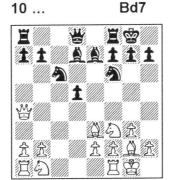

Perhaps the most natural.

11 Nc3   h6

11...Na5 12 Qc2 Nc4 13 Bd4 could transpose into the game after Black plays 13...h6 to avoid 13...Rc8 14 Ng5! which threatens mate at h7.

Black can also try 12...Rc8 immediately and then 13 Rad1 Bg4 with the idea of sacrificing the d-pawn after 14 Ng5 h6!? then 15 R×d5 Qc7! is very risky for White (*15 Qa4 Nc4*) as is 15 B×d5!? h×g5 16 B×f7ch R×f7 17 R×d8ch R×d8. But the strength of White's opening lies in pressure on *d5*, not necessarily a quick capture there. He gets a good game with the simple retreat 15 Nh3 after which 15...Bc5 16 B×c5 R×c5 17 Nf4 d4 18 h3 Bf5 19 Qa4 Rc4 20 Qa3 yields continuing Queenside pressure (Suba-Huebner, Thessaloniki 1984).

12 Rac1   Na5

(see diagram on next page)

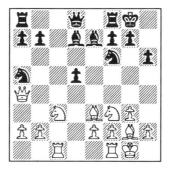

12...Nb4 13 Qb3 is excellent for White and 12...Ne5 13 Qb3 is also good.

13 Qc2	Nc4
14 Bd4	Be6

Here the game Suba-Balashov, Malta 1980 was drawn, but White can surely play for advantage with 15 b3, e.g., 15...Nd6 16 Na4 Bf5 17 Qb2.

E23

(1 c4 e5 2 g3 Nf6 3 Bg2 c6 4 d4 e×d4 5 Q×d4 d5 6 c×d5 c×d5 7 Nf3 Nc6 8 Qa4 Be7 9 0-0 0-0 10 Be3)

10 ...	Re8

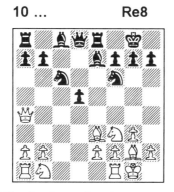

Similar to what Black does in the related position of the Queen's Gambit Declined, Tarrasch Variation.

11 Nc3	Bb4

Played apparently to pin White's Bishop to his e-pawn; on 11...Bg4 12 Rad1 Qd7 White has great pressure with 13 Bg5.

12 Rad1   R×e3?!

Obvious concern about 13 Nd4 which would have given White a rather clear advantage.

13 f×e3   Qe7
14 N×d5!   N×d5
15 R×d5   Be6
16 Rb5   Bc4

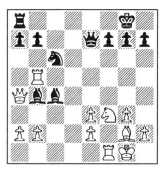

So far as in the game Hansen-Ligterink, Malta 1980 which continued 17 R×b7! Q×b7 18 Nd4 Bd2 19 Q×c4 B×e3ch 20 Kh1 B×d4 21 R×f7! Qb4 (*21...Q×f7 22 Bd5*) 22 Qe6 Kh8 23 B×c6.

CONCLUSION

Black's most popular 1...e5 systems against the English have been taken away by the strange White move order and his best prospects involve an early d7-d5, with or without the c6 preparation.   But in any case, White emerges with obvious positional trumps.

SECTION II
SYMMETRICAL SYSTEMS

1 c4　　　　c5

The most immediate problem with 1...c5, from White's point of view, is breaking out of a symmetrical pattern that may end up drawish. The symmetrical English has, in fact, become one of the most notorious drawing variations of modern International chess. When two GMs want to take the day off, they play c4, Nc3, fianchetto their KBs and prepare to shake hands.

Actually there is a lot more life to the positions arising after 1...c5 than first appears significant. Players such as Ulf Andersson have milked the Symmetrical English (with either side) for many years. Skill in the endgame — one of Andersson's chief attributes — is not essential to score in this variation. But it helps.

For the sake of clarity and to avoid some transpositional complications, we'll examine an opening sequence similar to what we saw after 1 c4 e5:

2 g3

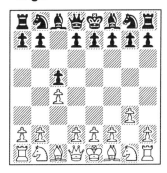

Black has considerable choice and we'll consider the following:

A	2...e6 with d5
B	2...Nf6 3 Bg2, e6 with b7-b6
C	2...Nf6 3 Bg2, d5
D	2...g6

The move orders in many cases do not matter, but in others they do a great deal. It will depend on the variation. For example, 2...e5 is an independent variation provided that Black doesn't play either a subsequent d5 leading into (C) nor g6 leading into (D). But such a sideline is bound to be suspicious, e.g., 3 Bg2 Nc6 4 Nc3 and now 4...f5 leads to a favorable position for White, for example: 5 e3 Nf6 6 Nge2 Be7 7 0-0 0-0 8 a3 d6 9 Rb1 a5 (else b2-b4 with an initiative) 10 d3 followed by Nd5, Bd2 and b2-b4. The Black pawn at *c5* only serves to encourage White's Queenside play in this case.

A

(1 c4 c5 2 g3)

2 ...   e6

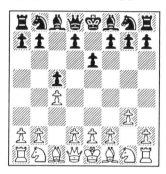

Black's intention here is usually to obtain freedom for his pieces at small positional cost, such as the price of an isolated d-pawn after 3 Nf3 d5 4 c×d5 e×d5 5 d4 (and a later d4×c5) or 3...Nf6 4 Bg2 d5 5 c×d5 N×d5 6 Nc3 Nc6 7 N×d5 e×d5 8 d4. This would result in a position similar to that reached in (E) of Section I. But we have a simpler policy to recommend for White.

3 b3

White's plan is to fianchetto both Bishops and ultimately exchange on *d5* after Black advances a pawn to that square. Then White will prepare his own d4, a move that will liquidate the remaining pawns in the center and (hopefully) result in a middlegame in which White's two Bishops scissor the board from opposite wings. This plan will be repeated in similar lines.

3 ...   d5

3...Nf6 4 Bb2 d5 or 3...Nc6 4 Bb2 Nf6 5 Bg2 d5 will transpose. Sometimes in the English, one gets the impression that everything transposes.

But 3...b6 does not. However, it is such a clumsy move (*4 Bg2 Nc6 5 Bb2* followed by *e3* and *d4!*) that we can safely ignore it.

4 Bb2

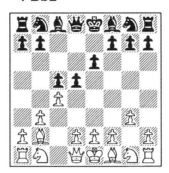

This is the first of several instances in which Black can set up a Benoni-like pawn structure with d5-d4. That move will severely limit one of White's prize Bishops. But at the same time, it liberates the other Bishop and gives White a target to shoot at on the d-file.

A typical continuation after 4...d4 would be 5 e3 Nc6 6 e×d4. Black could have advanced the pawn to *d3* (where it would have become encircled by an eventual Qb1 and Ne1) or exchange it off on *e6* (thus giving White a nice pawn center with d2-d4). His decision to permit an exchange on *d4* is sound, but perhaps not enough to equalize. After 6...N×d4 7 Nf3 N×f3ch 8 Q×f3 White has excellent power on the diagonals and will eliminate his backward d-pawn with a subsequent Rd1 and d2-d4. If instead 7...Nf6 8 Bg2 Be7 9 0-0 0-0 White obtains a good game with 10 N×d4 c×d4 11 Re1! thereby depriving Black of the e5 move needed to get his pieces coordinated. It's easy to see after 11 Re1 that 11...Qc7 and 11...Nd7 both designed to promote 12...e5, lose the d-pawn.

Better is 6...c×d4 7 Nf3 Nf6 8 Bg2 e5 but White again has a good game with 9 0-0 Be7 10 Re1, e.g., 10...e4 11 Ng5 or 10...Qc7 11 Na3.

4 ...   Nf6

There is nothing to be gained immediately from 4...d×c4 since White will get the exclusive use of the long white-squared diagonal from his *g2* to *b7* after 5 b×c4 and 6 Bg2. The exchange on *c4* will be explored further in the note to moves 7 and 9.

5 Bg2	Be7
6 Nf3	0-0
7 0-0	

There are several orders of moves to reach this position and several additional ones to reach the subsequent diagrams. The reason we have delayed considering Nc3 so far is because Black can play Nbd7. This is a worthwhile development since regardless of where Black puts his QN, he will develop his QB on *b7*. And since a Knight on *c6* blocks in the Bishop on *b7*, we must examine the alternatives. Here for example is 7...b6 8 Nc3 Bb7 9 e3! and now:

(Analysis diagram after 9 e3!)

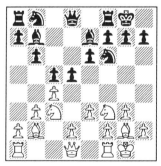

White is preparing for Qe2 followed by Rac1/Rfd1 and d2-d4. If Black plays 9...Nc6, he will transpose into the main line of the pages that follow this one. Suppose he plays 9...Nbd7 instead. Then 10 Rc1 is a useful move because Black has no good square for his Queen, e.g., 10...Qc7 11 c×d5 e×d5 12 d4 Rfd8 13 d×c5 b×c5 14 Qe2 with good play against the hanging center pawns. Or 11...N×d5 12 d4 Rad8 13 N×d5 B×d5 14 d×c5 b×c5 15 Qe2 as in Ivkov-Medina, Malaga 1969.

Black can avoid the center pawn weaknesses by playing 9...d×c4 first and then 10 b×c4 Nbd7. But after 11 Qe2 White is ready to shoot the center he has inherited by advancing up the board with d4-d5. He can also attack on the Queenside with a4-a5 as in the game Geller-Matanovic, Belgrade 1969 (*11...Ne4 12 N×e4 B×e4 13 d3 Bc6 14 a4! Bf6 15 Rfb1 B×b2 16 R×b2 Qf6 17 a5* weakening Black's Queenside).

7 ...	**Nc6**
8 e3!	

As explained earlier, White is preparing for Qe2/ Nc3/Rfd1 and a well-timed c×d5 followed by d2-d4.

He need not worry about 8...d4 because this is the Benoni we examined earlier. (*9 e×d4 N×d4 10 N×d4 c×d4* is no improvement, e.g., *11 Re1! Bc5 12 d3 Qc7 13 Nd2!* and *14 Nf3*).

If Black keeps the set of Knights on board with 9...c×d4 but delays advancing his e-pawn (*10 Re1 Re8 11 d3 Bc5 12 Nbd2 e5*), then White shifts from the assault on *e5* to Kingside pressure: 13 a3 a5 14 Ng5! Bf8 15 Nde4 N×e4 16 N×e4 Bf5 17 h3 f6 18 Bc1! and in Panno-Cifuentes, Argentina 1984 White was ready to expand with advantage — 18...Qd7 19 g4! and f4.

Black should realize in this variation that it is difficult to advance in the center. A delayed version of this is 8...Qb6 9 d3 Rd8 10 Qe2 Bd7 11 Nc3 and even now 11...d4 is questionable. In Bilek-Santo-Roman, Lille 1985 White played 12 Na4 Qa5 13 Rae1 after which Black liquidated his newly created center (*13...dxe3 14 fxe3 Nb4*) but found that White could play aggressively with 15 Ne5! bxa4 16 bxa4 Qxa4 17 a3 Nc6 18 Ng4 Nxg4 19 Qxg4 Bf8 20 Be4!, White has a fierce attack (*20...Rd7 21 Rf6! Qc2 22 Qh4 h6 23 Rxh6!* or *22...g6 23 Rf2 Qa4 24 Bxg6! fxg6 25 Qf6*).

Nor should he worry about Black's attempts to seize the long black-squared diagonal with 8...Ne4 and 9...Bf6. A good line for White is the simple 8...Ne4 9 cxd5 exd5 10 d3 Bf6 (*10...Nf6 11 d4!* or *10...Nd6 11 Nc3*) 11 Qc1! Bxb2 12 Qxb2 and Black's c-pawn is weak.

There are several other moves at this point (*8...Qa5, 8...Bd7, 8...Re8*) but they fail to solve the problem of Black's QB, e.g., 8...Bd7 9 Nc3 Rc8 10 cxd5 Nxd5 11 Nxd5 exd5 12 Rc1 Bg4 13 h3 and 14 d4.

| 8 ... | b6 |
| 9 Nc3 | Bb7 |

Here 9...d4? simply loses a pawn (*10 exd4 cxd4 11 Nxd4*). The Bishop tends to be misplaced on *a6* (*9...Ba6*) and White can defend his c-pawn with his Queen or even play 10 Nb5.

A more important alternative is 9...d×c4 10 b×c4 Bb7 in order to leave White with "hanging" central pawns before White can do the same for Black.

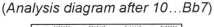

(Analysis diagram after 10...Bb7)

Now with 11 Qe2 White begins his middle strategy of advancing in the center. His d-pawn will be supported by a Rook while his c-pawn gets the protection of White's Queen (and, after Na5, also by a Knight on *e5*). The greatest threat White has is the long-term one of a breakthrough in the center, such as following 11 Qe2 Rc8 12 Rfd1 Qd7?! 13 d4 c×d4 14 e×d4 Rfd8 15 Ne5 or 15 d5.

It's safer for the Black queen on *c7* — but not entirely safe on 12...Qc7 13 Rac1 Rfd8 14 d4 Na5 White gets his breakthrough from 15 Nb5 Qb8 16 d5!, e.g., 16...e×d5 17 Be5 Qa8 18 Nc7 or 16...a6 17 Be5 Qa8 18 Nc7 Qa7 19 Bh3 and now in the brilliant game Mohring-Polojowczyk, Balatonbereny 1983, White won after 19...Nd7 20 d×e6 B×f3 21 e×f7ch Kh8 22 R×d7!! B×e2 23 R×e7 with crushing threats of 24 Ne6 (and *25 B×g7 mate*) and 24 Ne8 (and queening the pawn). A case of White's powerful pieces exploding.

Perhaps the safest policy for Black is to meet 11 Qe2 with 11...Qc7 12 Rfd1 a6 (avoiding Nb5). Then 13 Rab1 retains the possibility of pressure on *b6* as well as of a delayed advance of the d-pawn. In recent years, White has achieved excellent play in games that continued 13...Rab8 14 Ba1 Rfd8 15 d3 Na7 16 d4! c×d4 17 e×d4 b5 18 d5!? with immense complications.

Black can try to get by without ...a6 in this last line because Nb5 in itself is not a threat. However, the knight move is tactically dangerous as a support for the d-pawn's advance. For example, 12...Rfd8 (instead of *12...a6*) 13 Rac1 Rac8 coordinates Black's heavy pieces but allows 14 d4!. A key point is that 14...cxd4 15 exd4 Na5, attacking the c4-pawn, can be strongly met by 16 Nb5! and 17 d5. Much better is 14...Na5 immediately, but even after 15 Nb5, Bxf3! 16 Bxf3 Qb8 17 d5 White has a considerable advantage (Damljanovic-Yermolinsky, Moscow Olympiad 1994).

White's position after 11 Qe2 is promising because of his hanging pawns. Yet we'll examine a position in the main line in which Black is in trouble because he accepts the same hanging pawns. Why the difference? In part, this is due to White's slight lead in development and his more aggressively posted QB. The role of this Bishop becomes greater in the next several moves.

10 cxd5   Nxd5

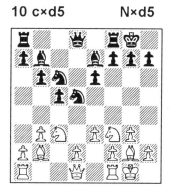

It is in Black's interest to get rid of one pair of Knights for several reasons. One is that after a subsequent d2-d4 by White, Black will be able to post his KB nicely at *f6* if it is vacant. The Black d-pawn may also be more easily defended after an exchange of pieces.

For example 10...exd5 11 d4 Qd7 looks reasonable for Black, but runs into immediate trouble after 12 Rc1. Then Black has difficulty covering his pawn weaknesses, e.g., 12...Rfd8 13 dxc5 bxc5 14 Na4 Ne4 15 Nd2! Geller-van Scheltinga, Wijk aan Zee 1969 or 12...Rac8 13 Ne5 Qe6 14 Ne2 Rfd8 15 Nf4 Qd6 16 Re1 Nb8 17 Nh5! with pressure on the Kingside as well, Csom-Miles, Bad Lauterburg, 1977.

11 N×d5

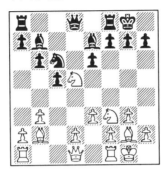

Black now makes his big decision of the opening, and it will determine the course of the middlegame. If he recaptures with a pawn, White plays 12 d4 and takes aim at the enemy center. On the other hand, if Black recaptures with his Queen, keeping his center relatively clear of pawns, he risks a liquidation of minor pieces (after d4 and Ne5 for instance) that will give White more active Rooks and minor pieces. We examine:

    A1   11...Q×d5
    A2   11...e×d5

A1

(1 c4 c5 2 g3 e6 3 b3 d5 4 Bb2 Nf6 5 Bg2 Be7 6 Nf3 0-0 7 0-0 Nc6 8 e3 b6 9 Nc3 Bb7 10 c×d5 N×d5 11 N×d5)

11 ...	**Q×d5**

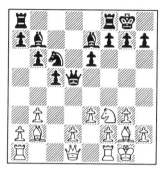

12 d4

Now 12...c×d4 loses material to 13 N×d4 and 14 N×c6.

12 ...	**Rfd8**

A natural move but 12...Rad8 13 Ne5 Qd6 14 N×c6 B×c6 15 Qg4! favors White slightly. Another idea is 12...Nb4, opening the diagonal so that 13 Ne5?? would be punished big time (*13...Q×g2 mate*). but White can still obtain an edge by forcing an endgame with 13 Nh4 Qd7 14 d×c5 Q×d1 15 Rf×d1 B×g2 16 K×g2 B×c5 17 a3 Nd5 (Nogueiras-J. Arencibia, Cuban Championship 1991). He expands with 18 b4 Be7 19 Nf5! e×f5 20 R×d5 or 19...Bf6 20 B×f6 N×f6 21 Ne7ch and 22 Rac1, as pointed out by Nogueiras.

13 Ne5!	**Qd6**
14 Qh5!	**g6**
15 Qf3	

(see diagram on next page)

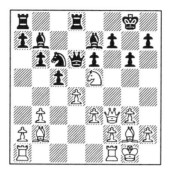

White obtains two beautiful Bishops which come in handy.

15 ...	N×e5
16 Q×b7	Nd3
17 d×c5	b×c5

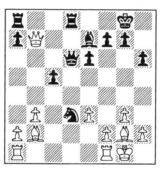

In the game Panchenko-Lengyel, Sochi 1981 Black tried 17...N×c5?!, but after 18 Q×a8! R×a8 19 B×a8 Qd2 20 Bd4 White's material edge was decisive. The game continued 20...a5 21 Bf3 h5 22 Rfd1 Qc2 23 Rac1 Qf5 (Not *23...Q×a2 24 b4 a×b4 25 Ra1* heading for h8 and mate) 24 Be2 Bf6 25 R×c5!, and Black is lost after 25...b×c5 26 e4 Q×e4 (or *26...Qg5 27 h4*) 27 B×f6 Q×e2 28 Rd8ch.

18 Bc3

And White will follow up with Rfd1 with fine chances.

A2

(1 c4 c5 2 g3 e6 3 b3 d5 4 Bb2 Nf6 5 Bg2 Be7 6 Nf3 0-0 7 0-0 Nc6 8 e3 b6 9 Nc3 Bb7 10 c×d5 N×d5 11 N×d5)

11 ...　　　　　e×d5

12 d4

Intending 13 Qd2 and 14 Rfd1 to win the d-pawn.

12 ...　　　　　a5

A counterattacking move against the Queenside so that Black can play a4-a×b3 and Nb4.

13 d×c5　　　　b×c5

13...B×c5 leads to a classic isolated d-pawn situation after 14 Nd4 Ne7 15 Qg4 and 16 Rfd1.

14 Nh4!　　　　B×h4
15 g×h4　　　　Q×h4

Otherwise the center pawns fall without compensation, e.g., 15...Ne7 16 Qg4 f6 17 Rac1 Rc8 18 Ba3 Qb6 19 Qd7! Rc7 20 B×c5!.

	16 Q×d5	Rae8

With Re6-g6 in mind.

	17 Qc4!	Qg5
	18 Qf4	

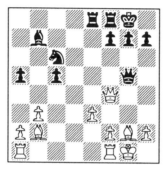

White obtains a superior endgame. The game Makarichev-Panchenko, USSR 1981 went 18...Q×f4 19 e×f4 Rb8 20 Rfc1 Nd4 21 B×d4! c×d4 22 Rc4 d3 23 Rd1 B×g2 24 K×g2 Rbd8 25 Rc3 Rd4 26 Rc×d3 R×f4 27 Rd4 R×d4 28 R×d4 Rb8 29 Rd5 a4 (On *29...Ra8* White has *30 Kf3* followed by going to the Queenside) 30 b4! a3 31 b5 Kf8 32 Kf3 Ke7 33 Ke4 Rc8 34 Rd3 and Black resigned in a few moves.

B

(1 c4 c5 2 g3 Nf6 3 Bg2 e6)

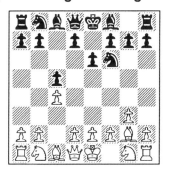

White's order of moves enables him to avoid some problem-some alternative systems often employed by Black. He may avoid, for example, the typical Queen's Indian systems that Black sets up as if playing against 1 d4.

Note for example that Black cannot play 3...b6 nor 3...g6 because of dangers along the diagonal that White controls first. White will have to block the diagonal temporarily with Nf3 but, as we'll see, Black is still denied *b6*.

4 Nf3

Now 4...b6 walks into 5 Ne5! d5 6 Nc3 followed by a check at a4, e.g., 6...Bd6 7 Qa4ch Nbd7 8 Nc6! or 7...Nfd7 8 cxd5! Bxe5 9 dxe6 Bxc3 10 exd7ch or 10 dxc3.

This may look simple, but a similar version occurred on Board 1 of the 1987 New York Open in the game Seirawan-Ftacnik which went 4...b6 5 Ne5 d5 6 cxd5 Nxd5 7 Nc3 Bb7 8 Qa4ch Nd7 9 Nxd5 Bxd5 10 Bxd5 exd5 11 Qc6 with advantage (1-0, 48).

4 ...   Nc6

(see diagram on next page)

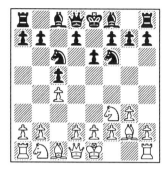

If Black plays 4...Be7 5 0-0 0-0 6 b3 b6 he can get his fianchetto in without entering the Subsection (A) lines with d5. There would follow 7 Bb2 Bb7 8 Nc3 and now 8...d5 transposes into (A) so Black must seek independent status with something like 8...Nc6 or 8...d6. The drawback to this is that in the absence of d6 by Black, White may usurp the center with his own pawns (*8...Nc6 9 e3 Rc8 10 Qe2 Qc7 11 Rac1 Rfd8 12 Rfd1* followed by *13 d4 c×d4 14 e×d4* with a slight edge for White because of his better placed Queen and superior minor pieces).

5 0-0   b6

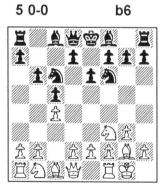

Now White can play into the previous note with 6 b3, but he has a more effective plan.

6 d3!

By setting up pawns at *d3* and *e4*, White shuts out the enemy fianchetto at the cost of limiting his own. But he reaches a middlegame in which he can open the position with e4-e5 or d2-d4, whereas Black has only d7-d5, a difficult to achieve advance. White keeps the initiative in this manner.

6 ...	Bb7
7 e4	

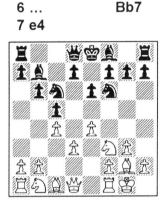

Notice that 7...d5 would expose Black to a fierce attack in the center after 8 c×d5 e×d5 9 e5!, e.g., 9...Ng4 10 h3 Ng×e5? 11 N×e5 N×e5 12 Re1 or 9...Nd7 10 d4 followed by Nc3 and Re1 (*10...c×d4 11 N×d4 Nc×e5? 12 Re1 and f2-f4 or Nf5, or 11...Nd×e5 12 N×c6 B×c6 13 Re1*).

7 ...	Be7
8 Nc3	0-0

Black still cannot play 8...d5 without considerable risk (*9 c×d5 e×d5 10 e5 Nd7 11 N×d5 Nd×e5 12 N×e7 N×f3ch 13 Q×f3 Q×e7 14 Q×c6ch! B×c6 15 B×c6ch and 16 B×a8 or 10...Ng4 11 Re1 d4 12 Ne4 Ng×e5 13 N×e5 N×e5 14 Bf4*).

9 b3

This enables White to take advantage of an opened center in case of a delayed e4-e5 or d3-d4 (or even d7-d5 by Black). The immediate 9...d5 is still very risky.

9 ...	d6
10 Bb2	

(see diagram on next page)

Here Black must come to a conclusion about the center. On 10...Rc8 or 10...Qc7 or some routine move such as that, White will play 11 d4!. But on 10...e5 White continues by moving his KN and playing for f2-f4, e.g., 11 Nh4 (or 11 Ne1-c2-e3-d5), Nd4 12 f4 Ne8 13 Nf5 with a slight edge. In either case, White has all the leverage and the better chances of activating his heavy pieces on ambitious squares.

C

(1 c4 c5 2 g3 Nf6 3 Bg2 d5)

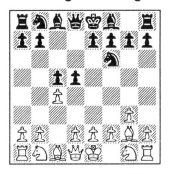

Note that this is the last moment Black can achieve the "Maroczy Bind Reversed" position he is seeking. If, instead, he plays 3...e5 (or *3...g6*) with the idea of following up with a subsequent d7-d5, White stops him with 4 Nc3. The White Knight is effective on *c3* in general, but especially when it is inconvenient or impossible for Black to play e6 and d7-d5-d4.

Black can play 3...Nc6 keeping the Maroczy option open, as well as the opportunity of meeting 4 Nc3 with 4...e6 and 5...d5 as in Subsection A. White can avoid that, if he prefers, by playing 4 Nf3, a move that leads back into our main line after 4...d5 5 c×d5 N×d5 6 Nc3 Nc7.

4 c×d5   N×d5

The ambition behind Black's last two moves is great: he seeks nothing less than the domination of the center by way of Nc6 and e5 and placement of Bishops at *e7* and *e6*. In this way,

White's central counterplay — the d2-d4 of Subsection A, for example — is put to rest and he must try to get room for his Rooks by way of f2-f4 or b2-b4. Black's Knights have futures at *d4* and *b4* as well.

But White has the initiative of the first move and with the use of positional threats, he can keep Black busy until well into the middlegame.

5 Nc3

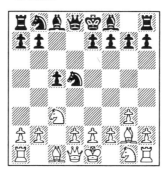

The first step is to gain some time in the center. Black has only one move that can be considered "developing" which also meets the threat to the Knight. This is 5...e6 which enables White to head back into Subsection (A) with 6 Nf3 Nc6 7 0-0.

But actually 5...e6?, although a seemingly natural move, and one often played by Masters (e.g., Bass-Dlugy, Bermuda 1984) is actually a blunder that loses a pawn. After 6 N×d5 e×d5 7 Qb3! Black cannot defend both *d5* and *b7* (*7...c4 8 Qb5ch!*)

Therefore Black's knight <u>must</u> move!

There are five moves by the Black Knight to be considered. (A sixth move *5...Be6?*, has the defect of leaving b7 unprotected and this can be exploited tactically by *6 Qb3 N×c3 7 Q×c3* attacking two pawns or *6...Nf4?? 7 Qa4ch*). The Knight moves are:

    C1   5...N×c3
    C2   5...Nb6

C3   5...Nb4
C4   5...Nf6
C5   5...Nc7

C1

(1 c4 c5 2 g3 Nf6 3 Bg2 d5 4 c×d5 N×d5 5 Nc3)

5 ...   N×c3

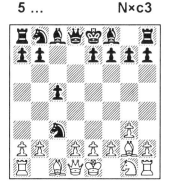

6 b×c3

This opens White's b-file and gives him an extra pawn in the center. He can use both advantages after 6...e5 by playing 7 Nf3 Nc6 8 0-0 Be7 9 d3 followed by Nd2 Rb1 and c3-c4!

6 ...   g6
7 Rb1

Creating troublesome pressure on *b7*.

7 ...   Qc7
8 Qa4ch   Nd7

On 8...Nc6 9 Ba3 is very strong.

    9 Nf3   **Bg7**
    10 d4!

Exposing the Queen to danger along the c-file and preparing to pound the Queenside. This explains one difference between 5...N×c3 in this variation and 5...N×c3 in the line we examined earlier with 1...e5 rather than 1...c5. The advanced Black c-pawn gives more space to him to withstand queenside pressure. But it also enables White to expand in the center more forcefully.

C2

(1 c4 c5 2 g3 Nf6 3 Bg2 d5 4 c×d5 N×d5 5 Nc3)

    5 ...   **Nb6**

A move that is useful when there is a Black pawn at *e5* rather than *c5*. It has one major disadvantage when compared with

5...Nc7 and that is its usefulness in confronting an attack on the Black c-pawn.

6 d3   e5

6...c4 is strongly answered by 7 d4!.

7 Be3   Be7
8 Rc1

White intends Ne4 and N×c5 and Black has no convenient method of meeting the threat. (Compare this with *5...Nc7* when Black can always bring the Knight to *e6*).

8 ...   0-0

Neither is 8...Na6 good because then 9 Nf3 (or *9 f4!?*) creates a problem for the e-pawn as well as the c-pawn (*9...f6 10 Nd2*, or *10 Qb3* to stop Black from castling)

9 Ne4

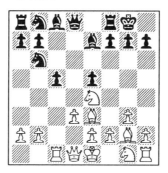

And now Black is forced into the doubtful 9...f5 10 N×c5 f4 11 Bd2. As the turn-of-the-century analyst George Marco said, "A Knight on *b6* is always poorly placed."

C3

(1 c4 c5 2 g3 Nf6 3 Bg2 d5 4 c×d5 N×d5 5 Nc3)

5 ...	Nb4

This puts the Black Knight offsides with little immediate prospect of getting back into action. There is no urgency to help Black out with a2-a3 because White will not be able to enforce b2-b4 afterwards. Instead, he should employ a simple maneuver that works very well in the reversed Maroczy.

6 Nf3	Nbc6
7 0-0	e5

Black can decide against the ambitious e7-e5 strategy by playing 7...g6, but there is bound to be counter chances for White involving attacks on the c-pawn or with the b2-b4 advance. For instance, 8 a3 Na6 9 b4!? c×b4 10 a×b4 Na×b4 11 Ba3 Bg7 12 Rb1 or, more accurately, 9 Ne1 (Threatening B×c6ch again) 9...Bd7 10 Nd3 Bg7 11 b4.

8 d3	Be7
9 Nd2!	

(see diagram on next page)

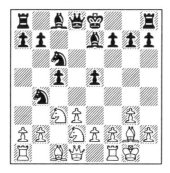

There is a positional threat here of 10 a3 Na6 11 B×c6ch! and 12 Nc4. Black's pawns in the center, all of them, are richly vulnerable to attack. White can then pound the c-pawn with moves like Rc1 and Ne4.

9 ...	Bd7

To meet the B×c6 threat.

10 a3	Na6
11 Nc4	

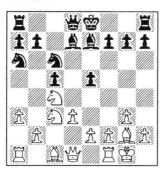

Now White threatens 12 B×c6 and 13 N×e4, winning the e-pawn, and invites the profitable liquidation of the center following 11...f6 12 f4! e×f4 13 B×f4.

C4

(1 c4 c5 2 g3 Nf6 3 Bg2 d5 4 c×d5 N×d5 5 Nc3)

5 ...   Nf6

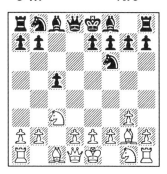

This doesn't fit in with the Maroczy ambitions either, since Black usually has to strengthen his pawn when it reaches *e5* with f6 or Bf6. The Knight on *f6* also leaves the wholly undeveloped Queenside susceptible to raids such as 6 Qb3!.

6 Qb3!   Nc6

This allows B×c6, but alternatives are also rather depressing. 6...Qc7 invites attacks on the c-pawn such as 7 Nf3 Nc6 8 Qb5 when 8...e6 (or *8...e5*) are met by 9 Ne5 (*9...Q×e5 10 B×c6ch*) and 9 N×e5 respectively.   Also 6...Nbd7 can be played because of the pin 7 B×b7? Rb8. However, Black's Knight is hardly happy at d7 (*7 Nf3 e5 8 Ng5! Qe7 9 Nb5* or *7...g6 8 Ng5 e6 9 Nge4*).

7 B×c6ch!   b×c6
8 Nf3

(see diagram on next page)

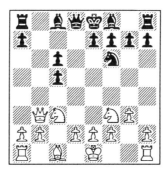

White has a terrific game, Ne5 being the immediate threat, and 8...Be6 9 Qa4 Qb6 10 d3 g6 11 Nd2 being one of the dangerous ways for Black to proceed-Nc4 and Be3 are coming up.

C5

(1 c4 c5 2 g3 Nf6 3 Bg2 d5 4 c×d5 N×d5 5 Nc3)

5 ...   Nc7

This Knight retreat is the best alternative, the rest of which fail to meet the power hungry demands of Black's ambitious plan.

6 Nf3

The Knight prepares *d4*, which would be a major breakthrough for the better developed side (*6...e6 7 d4 Nc6 8 Be3!*). The Knight also will be headed for the Queenside in order to attack Black's pawns — i.e., to *c4* via *d2* or *d3* via *e1*. Finally the Knight has some rapid deployment possibilities such as arise after 6...g6. Then 7 d4 is a reasonable move, but 7 Qa4ch! is much better: 7...Nc6 8 Ne5 wins at least a pawn; 7...Bd7 8 Qc4 has both 9 Q×c5 and 9 Ng5 threatened; 7...Qd7 8 Qc4 Nba6 leads to 9 Ne5! and 10 Qa4ch.

6 ...   Nc6

Almost a forced move considering what we've said above. The Knight gets to move because White's diagonal is blocked and B×c6ch is not possible.

7 0-0

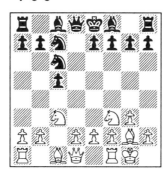

Again, White selects simple moves. His strategy will be based on what Black does at this point.

The strategies include:

(1) <u>The center punch - d4</u>. In connection with a frontal attack on the c-pawn, this can be dangerous if Black fails to play e7-e5. For example, 7...e6?! 8 d3 Be7 9 Be3 0-0 10 d4! and we have Kotov-R. Byrne from the 1954 USSR-US Radio Match which continued to White's advantage with 10...c×d4 11 N×d4 Nb4 12 N4b5! N×b5 13 N×b5.

(2) <u>The quiet buildup</u>. If White can draw some attention to Black's Queenside and other weaknesses, he can get time to concentrate his heavy pieces in the center with e3, Qe2 and the placement of Rooks on *d1* and *c1*. For example, 7...g6 8 Na4 Ne6 is one solid formation for Black (compare it with *8...b6* which invites the tactics of *9 d4! c×d4 10 Bf4* threatening *11 N×d4 N×d4 12 B×c7*, e.g., *10...Bg7 11 N×d4 N×d4 12 B×c7 Q×c7 13 B×a8 0-0 14 Nc3 Rd8 15 Bg2 Nf3ch 16 B×f3*

R×d1   17   Rf×d1 with a very nice position for White, Polugaevsky-Taimanov, USSR Championship 1967).

Since there is no way of breaking the solidity of Black's center after 8...Ne6, White can play quietly with 9 b3 Bg7 10 Bb2 B×b2 11 N×b2 0-0 12 e3.

(Analysis diagram after 12 e3)

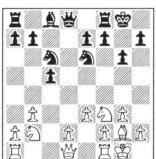

White has the only promising pawn break in the position, and it is d4, a move that requires only two moves of preparation. For a view of the future, consider 12...b6 13 Qe2 (*13 Ne5 N×e5 14 B×a8 Ba6*) 13...Bb7 14 Rfd1 Qd7 15 d4! How does Black avoid the pawn fork at his *d5*? The prospects are unpleasant. After 15...c×d4 16 e×d4, consider the following:

    a)   16...Nc7 17 Ne5!

    b)   16...Nc×d4 17 N×d4 N×d4 18 R×d4 Q×d4 19 B×b7

    c)   16...Na5 17 Ne5 Qd6 18 d5.

(3) The attack on the c-pawn. A typical case of this is one in which White also uses his other positional ideas, the capture on c6 and the break on the Kingside with f2-f4. For example, after 7...g6 8 Na4 e5 White plays 9 Ne1 which threatens both Nd3 and B×c6ch, while stopping 9...b5. After 9...Ne6 10 B×c6ch b×c6 11 b3 Ba6 12 Bb2 f6 (*12...Qc7 13 f4*) 13 Rc1 and 14 f4 White has nice thematic pressure against the various Black weaknesses. Better for Black is 9...Bd7, but then 10 Nd3 is annoying, e.g., 10...b6 11 f4 or 10...c4 11 Ndc5.

All these themes are available, but if Black plays accurately, White may be limited to the third.

7 ...   e5

This stops d4 by White once and for all, and reduces the effectiveness of any slow buildup. But he has several methods of hitting the c-pawn. We prefer:

8 Ne1!

White threatens B×c6ch before Black even gets to castle. It's important to realize that B×c6ch is not just an attempt to win the pawn that emerges on c6. The removal of the Black QN from the board also enables White to hit the more important pawns at *e5* and *c5*. For instance, 8...Be7 9 B×c6ch! b×c6 10 Qa4 and now 10...0-0 is playable since 11 Q×c6 Rb8 gives Black good play for an insignificant pawn (*12...Bb7* and Ne6-d4).

But White has the superior 11 b3, with the plan of Ba3 and Nd3, e.g., 11...Bh3 12 Ng2 Qd7 13 d3 f5 14 Ba3 Ne6 15 Qc4 and 16 Na4 or 14...f4 15 Ne4.

There is a similar story after 8...Bg4 which seeks to meet 9 Nd3 with 9...Q×d3! but which again permits 9 B×c6ch b×c6 10 Qa4, this time with greater effect (*10...Qd7 11 Nd3 f6 12 b3* and if *12...B×e2* then *13 N×e5 f×e5 14 N×e2* looks best).

8 ... Bd7

A wild, relatively untested idea here is 8...h5!?, trying to exploit the fact that White has castled and then removed the Kingside's best defensive piece. The threat is 9...h4 followed by 10...h×g3 11 h×g3 Qg5! and 12...Qh5.

It would be crazy for White to think of a purely positional plan — such as 9 B×c6ch — as an answer to 8...h5. A better idea is 9 f4 and then 9...h4 10 d3 h×g3 11 h×g3 as in the complex game Nikolic-Cebalo, Vrsac 1983, which led to White's advantage following 11...c4!? 12 d×c4 Bc5ch 13 e3 Q×d1 14 N×d1 e×f4 15 Nd3!? f3 16 R×f3 Be7 17 N1f2.

9 Nd3

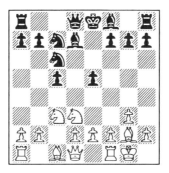

White is threatening the e-pawn (*10 B×c6* and *11 N×e5*). He need not go into a risky line of play since his Knight maneuver has pushed Black into a passive placement of his Bishop. For example, after 9...Be7 he can take chances with 10 B×c6 b×c6 (*10...B×c6 11 N×e5* "regains" the Bishop) 11 N×e5 Bh3

12 N×c6! Qd7 13 N×e7 B×f1 14 K×f1 Q×e7 15 Qa4ch Qd7 16 d3 as suggested by Watson, or play quietly with 10 b3 0-0 11 Bb2 b6 12 f4.

The one forcing line at Black's disposal is 9...c4 after which 10 B×c6 b×c6 11 N×e5 Bh3 is no good because of 12 Qa4! threatening a big check at c6. Instead, Black must play 10...c×d3 although he has little to show for a pawn after 11 B×b7 Rb8 12 Bg2 (*12...Bg4 13 f3*).

9 ...   f6
10 b3

Here Watson recommends 10...Bg4, reasoning that since White cannot play his Queen to *a4*, his 11 B×c6ch is not as strong as usual — even though White has an extra tempo. He says White is still better after 11 B×c6ch b×c6 12 f3 Bf5 13 Nf2! and we agree. A likely continuation would be 13...Be7 14 Na4 0-0 15 Ba3 Ne6 16 Rc1 Qa5 17 Ne4.

The chief alternative is 10...Be7 with possibilities such as 11 f4! e×f4 12 N×f4 0-0 13 Bb2 — now the Bishop has a future on this diagonal — 13...Rc8 14 e3! A Grandmaster game Vaganian-Lengyel, Moscow 1975 came to a speedy end after 14...b6 15 N3d5 Bd6 16 d4 Ne7? 17 d×c5 B×c5 18 b4! because the Bishop is caught on a bad square (*18...Nc×d5 19 B×d5ch*). Black's position was unpleasant in any case, and this game illustrates the theme of the f2-f4 break followed by Bb2 and e3 as well.

Having examined systems in which Black threatens to or actually goes ahead with d7-d5, we'll now concentrate on the last major alternative of the symmetrical English. This is when Black continues the symmetry as long as possible.

D

(1 c4 c5 2 g3)

2 ...   g6

If Black is going to fianchetto, he should do it this way (or after *2...Nc6*) in order to be the least committal with his pawn structure and KN. By bringing out his KN first (*2...Nf6*) he encourages White to play e3 and d4. We'll see this more clearly in a page or two.

3 Bg2   Bg7
4 e3!

This is an unusual order of moves (compared with Nc3 at the second, third, or fourth turn) but it has good points to it. Among the advantages are that Black avoids the controversial variation that arises after 4 Nc3 Nc6 5 e3 B×c3!? with complex play after 6 d×c3 d6 7 Ne2 Qd7 8 Nf4 b6 and 9...Bb7, or 6 b×c3 b6 7 Ne2 Bb7 8 d3 d6 and again Qd7, in each case with the possibility of 0-0-0.

There is no harm done from delaying Nc3 since Black is in no position to play d7-d5. When Black plays Nf6, White will respond Nc3.

4 ...   e6

(see diagram on next page)

Let's examine what happens if Black breaks the symmetry:

    D1   4...Nf6
    D2   4...e5
    D3   4...Nc6

D1

(1 c4 c5 2 g3 g6 3 Bg2 Bg7 4 e3)

    4 ...   **Nf6**

    5 Nc3   **Nc6**

Now 5...e6 or some other sequence involving ...e6 (i.e., 5...Nc6 6 Nge2 0-0) will lead back into our main line (4...e6).

    6 Nge2   **0-0**
    7 d4!

White seizes the initiative in the center with this thrust. Black must be careful about a slow build-up of enemy forces in the center involving b3, Bb2 and d4-d5 or d×c5 .

7 ...   d6

Black must avoid exchanging in the center himself because White will later be able to push his d-pawn to the fifth rank and clear a spot for his KN, e.g., 7...c×d4 8 e×d4 d6 9 0-0 Bf5 10 d5! Ne5 11 b3 and 12 Nd4 with a great game. White's Knight cannot be dislodged from *d4*, but Black faces danger on the e-file from Re1 and f2-f4.

8 0-0   Bd7

Black's plan of expanding on the Queenside with b7-b5 is his most active — in fact his only active idea. Other pawn action is bound to leave weaknesses (*8...e5? 9 d×c5 d×c5 10 b3* followed by *Ba3* and *Nd5*) or play into White's positional hands.

9 b3   a6

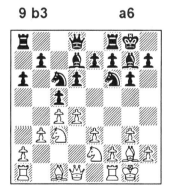

Weaker is 9...Qc8 10 Bb2 Bh3 11 d5! B×g2 12 K×g2 Na5 13 Qd2 when Black has traded off White's bad Bishop at some loss of time for himself.

10 Bb2	**Rb8**
11 Qd2	

Preparing to exploit the d-file.

11 ...	**b5**

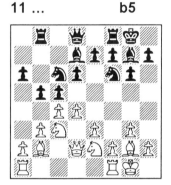

After 11...c×d4 12 e×d4 b5 13 c×b5 a×b5 14 d5! Na5 15 Nd4 - aiming at the weakened *c6* square, among others — gives White a clear advantage.

12 c×b5	**a×b5**
13 d×c5	**d×c5**
14 Rfd1	**Qb6**
15 Nf4	**e6**
16 Ne4!	

White has a positional advantage as Black's pawns are weak, Pytel·Kupke, Zagreb 1977.

The indications are that this 4...Nf6 is too passive and that Black might do better to stop d2-d4. This is considered under (D2) following, but for the moment look at 4...Nf6 5 Nc3 Nc6 6 Nge2 e5?! White can develop in the manner we'll examine shortly (*b3* and *Bb2*), but even here 7 d4 is promising, e.g., 7...e×d4 8 e×d4 d6 9 h3! stopping Bg4 and preparing Be3.

D2

(1 c4 c5 2 g3 g6 3 Bg2 Bg7 4 e3)

4 ...	e5

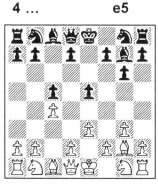

5 Ne2	Ne7
6 Nbc3	Nbc6

As pointed out above, when Black plays ...e7-e5 the only logical placement of his Knights is at *c6* and *e7* to deter d2-d4. Black is looking for d7-d5 himself, since that would expose White's center, especially his "backward" d-pawn, to attack. This means White must be prepared to occupy *d5* with a Knight when Black threatens to push his d-pawn.

7 0-0	0-0
8 b3	

(see diagram on next page)

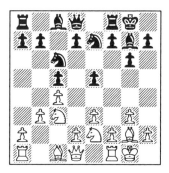

The thinking behind this move, which prepares Bb2, Qd2 and Rad1, goes this way: White needs to advance one of his pawns to the fourth rank to attack Black's *c5* or *e5* — otherwise Black will have time to make his own favorable liquidation of pawns with d7-d5 or b7-b5. White has been restrained by Black's piece and pawn placement from attempting d2-d4 — for the time being. He then must choose between b2-b4 and f2-f4. The choice is in favor of the latter because after he succeeds in playing b2-b4, Black cannot be prevented from playing b7-b5. This would clear the Queenside of two sets of pawns and since both sides are equally developed in that area, there is not likely to be any significant benefit to White.

So he aims for f2-f4.

8 ...   d6

This move is inevitable. If Black rushes forward with 8...a6 9 Bb2 Rb8 10 d3 b5 11 Qd2, he will have succeeded in reaching the main line by way of 11...d6.

9 Bb2   Rb8

(see diagram on next page)

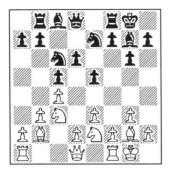

A nice point in White's favor is 9...Be6 10 Ne4! which is even better than 10 Nd5 in delaying d6-d5. After 10...f5 White drops his Knight onto g5 and continues with f2-f4, e.g., 11 Ng5 Bc8 12 f4 h6 13 Nh3 followed by d4. And on 10...h6 White has 11 d4 immediately, e.g., 11...f5 12 d5 or 11...e×d4 12 e×d4 f5 13 Nd2 c×d4?! 14 Nf3.

Notice that 9...f5 is no danger to White because he can forestall any Kingside intentions with 10 f4! followed ultimately with d4, after considerable preparation. There is nothing to be gained from 10...e4 since White favorably dissolves the enemy pawn chain with 11 d3 before Black gets to occupy *d3*.

10 d3	a6
11 Qd2	b5
12 Rad1	

White is not yet ready for a pawn advance in the center, but the time is fast approaching. His next set of preparatory moves include h3 and Kh2, so that he can follow up the eventual f2-f4 in some cases with g3-g4. The White QN will be going to *d5* as soon as Black plays his Bishop to e6, its best square (i.e., *12...Be6 13 Nd5 Qd7 14 f4* intending *15 f×e5* and *16 Nf6ch*). If Black occupies his *f5* with his KN White can put his own Knights at *e4* and *d5*, where they have considerable impact on the Black squares that will come under attack with f2-f4.

12 ...	Qa5

This was played in the most famous example of this line, Lein-Polugaevsky, Tiflis 1967, and it did not impress then. Clearly Black means to keep open the option of exchanging pawns on the Queenside while avoiding any immediate action there (...*b4?* closes up his most fruitful area of exploration and an immediate *12...b×c4 13 d×c4?!* dooms the d-pawn. Besides *12...Be6* mentioned above, there is *12...f5* with a likely continuation being *13 f4* (again) *Be6 14 Nd5* or *12...Bb7 13 Nd5* and *14 f4*).

13 h3   Be6
14 Ba1!

This last move clears the second rank and b-file so that there are never any attempts to grab the a-pawn with b5-b4 or to exploit the position of the Bishop with two captures on White's c4. In the 1967 stem game play continued: 14...f5 15 f4! Kh8 16 Qc1 (preparing to double Rooks on the d-file and play Nd5) 16...Nb4 17 Rd2 Bg8 18 Kh2 Rbd8 19 Rfd1 h6 20 a3 Nbc6 21 Nd5! and White had a very nice game. He was winning shortly after 21...N×d5 22 c×d5 Nb8 23 f×e5 d×e5 24 Q×c5.

D3

(1 c4 c5 2 g3 g6 3 Bg2 Bg7 4 e3)

4 ...	Nc6

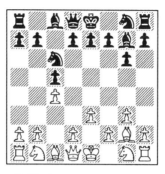

5 Ne2	Nh6

This system seeks to stop d2-d4 without blocking Black's diagonal with e7-e5 (the move that gave White f2-f4 and Nd5 in the last line). It is true that White can still play d2-d4, but he cannot maintain control of the d4 square (*6 d4?! c×d4 7 e×d4 Nf5 8 d5 Ne5 9 Na3 Nd6* or *8...Ncd4*).

However the placement of the Black Knight on *f5* makes the square *e4* an attractive outpost for White since a Knight there cannot be dislodged by enemy pawns. White has a simple plan similar to the one employed against e7-e5.

6 Nbc3	Nf5
7 0-0	0-0
8 b3!	

(see diagram on next page)

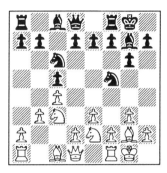

Again this development is effective, especially since the coming exchange of Black-squared Bishops will promote both d2-d4 and a potential Kingside attack. Two typical counterplans by Black are:

> **D31** 8...b6
> **D32** 8...a6

D31

(1 c4 c5 2 g3 g6 3 Bg2 Bg7 4 e3 Nc6 5 Ne2 Nh6 6 Nbc3 Nf5 7 0-0 0-0 8 b3)

8 ...	b6

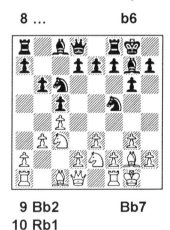

9 Bb2	Bb7
10 Rb1	

Protecting the Bishop and preparing Nd5 or Ne4.

10 ...	e6
11 Nf4	d6

12 Ne4!	B×b2
13 R×b2	Qe7
14 Qa1!	

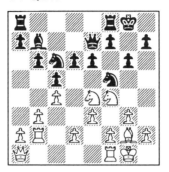

And White seizes the beautiful abandoned diagonal. A game Geller-R. Byrne, Sousse 1967, continued 14...Ng7 15 h4 f5 16 Ng5 and White blasted open the center with d4.

D32

(1 c4 c5 2 g3 g6 3 Bg2 Bg7 4 e3 Nc6 5 Ne2 Nh6 6 Nbc3 Nf5 7 0-0 0-0 8 b3)

8 ...	a6

9 Bb2	d6
10 d3	Rb8
11 Qd2	Bd7

As with the e7-e5 system, Black has insufficient counterplay along the b-file to compensate for the inevitable explosion in the center.

12 Ne4!	Qa5
13 Bc3	B×c3
14 N4×c3	b5
15 Rfe1	Rfc8
16 Rad1	

With d3-d4 coming up, White has a very nice position indeed; from the game Andersson-Miles, Tilburg 1977.

Returning back to our symmetry, we look for a safer alternative for Black. Everything we've seen so far allows an inevitable — and inevitably dangerous — d4 by White.

(1 c4 c5 2 g3 g6 3 Bg2 Bg7 4 e3 e6)

| 5 Ne2 | Ne7 |

This is the first of many positions in which Black can advance his own d-pawn. The danger to him, as well as to White if he advances prematurely, is that following an exchange of pawns, he may be stuck with an immobile isolated target on his d4/d5. For example, here 5...d5? would be met by 6 c×d5 e×d5 7 d4!. The threat is to win at least a pawn with 8 d×c5. After something like 7...Ne7, Black may keep the material balance briefly (*8 d×c5 Na6 9 Nbc3 Be6*) but his position is genuinely poor in the long run (*10 Nf4* or*10 Nd4*). No better is 7...c4 since then White can isolate the enemy d-pawn with 8 b3 or just pile up on it with 8 Nbc3 Ne7 9 Nf4.

This pattern may recur in different settings over the next few moves. So pay attention!

6 Nbc3   Nbc6

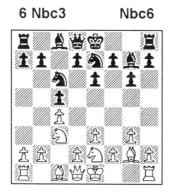

It's not much better to play d5 with a pair of Knights out, e.g., 6...d5?! 7 c×d5 N×d5 and now 8 N×d5 e×d5 9 d4 or the more aggressive 9 Qb3! (*9...c4 10 Qb5ch* and *11 Q×d5*).

7 d4!

This novelty, in connection with White's 11th move is a recent discovery of the Swedish star Ulf Andersson. It's advantage over the popular 7 0-0 0-0 8 d4 — a notorious drawing variation — will become apparent in a few moves. With 0-0 at any subsequent point, White can transpose into the more theoretically known positions and he should use this transposition only when it leads to advantage.

7 ...   c×d4

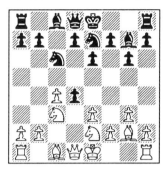

In contrast with 4...Nc6 5 Ne2 Nh6 mentioned earlier, White will make real progress if he can play d5, or d×c5, as follows:

7...b6? 8 d5! e×d5 9 N×d5 or 9 c×d5

7...d6? 8 d×c5 d×c5 9 Q×d8ch N×d8 10 Ne4.

8 N×d4

It is important to capture here with a Knight or Black will turn the tables with 8 e×d4 d5 when his Knights are as active as White's.

We now examine two main possibilities:

D32a 8...d5
D32b 8...N×d4

D32a

(1 c4 c5 2 g3 g6 3 Bg2 Bg7 4 e3 e6 5 Ne2 Ne7 6 Nbc3 Nbc6 7 d4 c×d4 8 N×d4)

8 ...   d5

This is necessary at some point to avoid being smothered in the center. After the natural 8...0-0 White may stop the enemy advances once and for all by exposing his Queen with 9 N4e2 (*9...d5 10 c×d5 e×d5 11 N×d5 N×d5 12 Q×d5*).

The advantage of 8...d5 rather than 8...N×d4 9 e×d4 d5 is that Black still has an active piece at *c6* which is tactically useful in defense.

9 c×d5   N×d5

Now 9...N×d4 10 e×d4 e×d5 11 0-0 0-0 12 Bg5! or 10...N×d5 11 0-0 0-0 12 Qb3! will transpose into lines mentioned above. Black hopes for dead equality from 10 N×d5 N×d4! 11 0-0 0-0 when White cannot win the enemy d-pawn without losing his own.

10 N×d5   N×d4

Again, 10...e×d5 can be met by 11 Ne2! exposing the d-pawn.

(see diagram on next page)

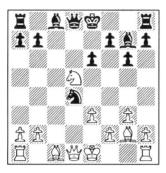

11 Nc3!

This leads out of symmetry and towards an endgame in which White will have the effect of two extra tempi. The first tempo comes from being White and having made the first move of the game. The second tempo comes from the slight disorienting effect of his next move, a check.

11 ...	Nc6
12 Q×d8ch	N×d8

If Black keeps his King in the center by way of 12...K×d8, White will continue as in the main line but with added effect when he brings his KR to the d-file.

13 Bd2

Despite appearances, the position is not easy for Black to play. The Soviet GM Sergei Makarichev cites an imitative line of play beginning with 13...Bd7, but concludes White is much better after 14 Ne4! Bc6 15 Nd6ch Kd7 16 B×c6ch K×d6 17 Bf3 B×b2 18 Rb1 and 19 Ke2, or 16...K×c6 17 Nc4.

Similarly 13...Ke7, which guards the d6 square, is risky because of 14 Rc1 Bd7 15 Ne4 intending Nc5 and Bb4ch.

13 ...   **0-0**
14 Rc1

The pawn structure is a mirror image and the pieces are likely to be traded off for one another, but White still holds an initiative. An indication of the difficulty Black faces is the game Andersson-Miles, Tilburg 1981 which saw Black ground down methodically: 14...Bd7 15 0-0 Bc6 16 Rc2 B×g2 17 K×g2 Nc6 18 Ne4 Rfd8 19 Bc3 Rac8 20 B×g7 K×g7 21 Rfc1 (intending *22 Nc5 b6 23 N×e6ch* or *22...Rc7 23 N×b7*) 21...Rb8 22 a3 a5 23 Rc3 f5 24 Nc5 Rd6 25 Rb3 b5 26 Rd3 R×d3 27 N×d3 Rb6 28 f4 Kf6 29 Kf3 e5 30 f×e5ch N×e5ch 31 N×e5 K×e5 32 Rc5ch Kd6?! 33 b4 Rb7 34 h4 a4 35 Kf4 Ke6 36 h5! Kf6 37 Rc6ch and White eventually penetrated with his King.

Anyone who wants to win regularly with the English should try to learn how to win endgames such as this. There is no real risk of losing and plenty of chances to take the full point.

D32b

**(1 c4 c5 2 g3 g6 3 Bg2 Bg7 4 e3 e6 5 Ne2 Ne7 6 Nbc3 Nbc6
7 d4 c×d4 8 N×d4)**

8 ...	N×d4

A major alternative to 8...d5.

9 e×d4	d5

Not 9...d6 because of 10 d5! with advantage for White.

10 c×d5!

Best.   After 10 c5 b6 is good for Black as 11 b4 allows
11...a5!.

10 ...	e×d5

On 10...N×d5 11 0-0 White's first move in the symmetrical
position is enough to count after 11...0-0 12 Qb3! B×d4 13
Bh6 Re8 14 Rad1 B×c3 15 b×c3 Qb6 16 Qc4 Qc6 17 Qe2 intending c4 or Qe5, Cardoso-Torre, Manila 1973.   Or 13...Bg7

(Instead of *13...Re8*) 14 B×g7 K×g7 15 Rfd1 Qb6 16 N×d5 with an obvious edge in the ending. Black can avoid some of the trouble in the center by disdaining the d-pawn, but 12...N×c3 13 b×c3 leaves him searching for a way to develop the Queenside 13...Rb8 14 Bf4; 13...Qe7 14 Ba3; 13...e5 14 d×e5 B×e5 15 Bh6 Re8 16 Rfe1. Also 12...Ne7 13 Rd1 is good for White (*13...B×d4? 14 Bg5*).

11 0-0		0-0
12 Bg5!		

Creating difficulties for Black in defending the d-pawn.

12 ...		Be6

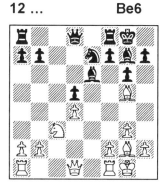

After 12...f6 13 Bf4 Be6 14 Re1 White holds a considerable edge (*14...Qd7 15 Qe2*).

13 Qb3	Qd7
14 B×e7!	Q×e7
15 B×d5	B×d4
16 Rae1	

(see diagram on next page)

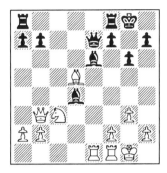

White has excellent chances, Hort-Spassky, Montreal 1979, which continued 16...Rae8 17 Re4 Qf6 18 B×e6 f×e6 19 Nb5!?.

CONCLUSION

After 1...c5 White's greatest difficulty may lie in meeting systems in which Black can play e6/d5/or g6. The typical advantages tend to be smaller for him than after 1...e5, but Black has fewer opportunities to make his own progress.

SECTION III

1 c4   Nf6

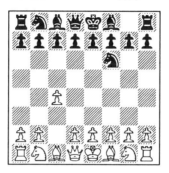

This is a transpositional move with only a few independent lines to consider. The possible jumps and hops into other variations are so many that the regular English player must have a concrete repertoire laid out for himself. There are dangers of finding himself in a position he's never faced before. For example, 2 Nc3 in the diagram could be met by 2...e5, transposing into a version of Reversed Sicilian (usually reached by *1 c4 e5 2 Nc3 Nf6*) that we have not explored in Section I. Also, the other natural Knight move, while perfectly good, can land the careless opening strategist into unknown territories after 2...c5. (You won't find that position analyzed in Section II). For these and other reasons we'll examine:

2 g3

And these possible responses:

A   2...d5

B   2...g6 (also 2...d6)

C   2...e6

D   2...c6

Note that 2...e5 returns us to Section I and 2...c5 gets us back into Section II, both into positions now familiar.

A

(1 c4 Nf6 2 g3)

2 ...   d5

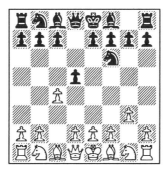

A move often effective after 2 Nc3 since after 3...N×d5 the Black Knight can exchange on *c3* rather than retreat.

3 c×d5   N×d5

3...Q×d5?! should be a loss of time after 4 Nf3, e.g., 4...Nc6 5 Nc3 Qh5 6 Qb3 or 4...e5 5 Nc3 Qa5 6 Bg2 Nc6 7 d3.

4 Bg2

This position takes on new meaning only if Black avoids 4...e5, seen already in Subsection E of Section I and 4...c5, which we disposed of in Subsection C of the last section.

4 ...   g6

Black can blaze new trails with 4...e6 5 Nc3 b6, but 6 Qa4ch Bd7 7 Qc4 is unpleasant and there isn't much promise in something like 5...Be7 6 Qb3.

5 Qb3!

(see diagram on next page)

A problemsome move because of the targets at *d5* and *b7* and the annoying prospect of Qc3 coming up. Clearly, 5...Nf6? 6 B×b7 and 5...Be6? 6 Q×b7 are unplayable, while 5...Nb6 6 Qc3! f6 7 h4 is very annoying (*7...Bg7 8 h5 0-0 9 h×g6 h×g6 10 Nf3 and 11 Nh4*).

| 5 ... | c6 |
| 6 e4 | |

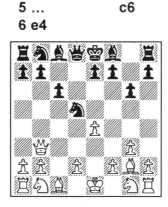

The most aggressive. Now if the Knight retreats to *b6* or *c7*, White continues with 7 Qc3 as in the line above.

| 6 ... | Nf6 |
| 7 Ne2 | |

And White will continue with 8 d4 and enjoy a very promising game. A likely sequence of moves into the middlegame would be 7...Bg7 8 d4 0-0 9 Nbc3 Qb6 10 Qa3, and 11 e5. Black can't stop d4 with 7...c5?, but 7...e5 isn't as bad (*8 Na3* is one answer but *8 0-0* and *9 Rd1* looks better).

B

(1 c4 Nf6 2 g3)

2 ...	g6

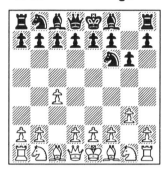

2...d6 and 3...g6 would lead to the same positions.

The King's Indian Defense can be played against any closed opening formation for White (*1 d4*; *1 c4*; *1 b3*; *1 f4*, etc.) and is perfectly reasonable here. To keep the "English" nature of the opening, we will examine in depth a system similar to the Botvinnik setup examined in A of Section I.

3 Bg2	Bg7
4 Nc3	0-0

It would do Black no good to try to get d7-d5 in earlier, e.g., 4...c6 5 e4 transposing into lines that follow. Note also that 4...e5 or 4...c5 will do the same.

5 e4	

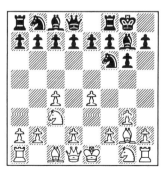

The Botvinnik system tends to work best when Black has played KN to *f6*, thereby cutting down control of White's *d4* from the Black Bishop at *g7*. Also, the natural King's Indian policy of e7-e5 can be met here by f2-f4-f5 by White since Black probably will not have time (it depends on the order of moves) to meet it with his own f7-f5.

5 ...   d6

Again Black may try c6 and d5, but with so much firepower concentrated on his *d5*, White will keep that sacrificed pawn for some time. For example, 5...c6 6 Nge2 d5?! 7 c×d5 c×d5 8 e×d5 Na6 9 0-0 Nb4 10 Nf4 Bf5 11 d3 and now Black must do something like 11...g5?! 12 Nh5 B×d3 13 Re1 Bg6 14 N×g7 K×g7 or 12...N×h5 13 Q×h5 h6 14 h4 Bg6 to get his pawn back. But he is obviously worse.

Best after 5...c6 6 Nge2 is 6...d6, reaching a position considered in the next note.

6 Nge2

There are three familiar policies in the King's Indian when White has played d2-d4. They are: e7-e5, c7-c5, and a flanking attack of c6, a6, and b7-b5. The latter will inevitably involve a delayed e7-e5 because otherwise Black has no impact on the center.

Black has three lines now:

B1   6...c6
B2   6...c5

B3   6...e5

With 6...Nbd7 Black delays a decision. But if he plays ...c5 later on, then his Knight will look silly on *d7* rather than *c6*.

B1

(1 c4 Nf6 2 g3 g6 3 Bg2 Bg7 4 Nc3 0-0 5 e4 d6 6 Nge2)

6 ...	c6

Hinting at ...b5 as well as ...d5.

7 0-0	a6
8 a4	a5

Black must play thus, both to justify the earlier move, and to avoid the restricting 9 a5. After 8...a5 Black has secured control of *b4* for his pieces and will be able to add *c5* as a second outpost when he eventually plays e7-e5. But White has a counter-strategy that severely tests Black.

9 h3

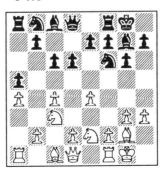

With the idea of dominating the center with 10 f4, 11 d4 and 12 e5. The reason for this particular sequence is that after 9...Nbd7 10 f4 he can meet 10...Qb6ch with 11 Kh1.

9 ...	Nbd7
10 f4	e5
11 f5	

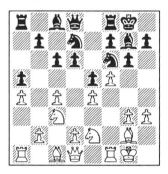

This is the kind of Kingside expansion White is looking for when he adopts the Botvinnik setup. White's d-pawn will now go modestly to *d3*, thereby avoiding the center tension of d4/...e5×d4 that would aid Black's counterplay. Black must take measures against the eventual g4-g5 or d3/Be3/Qd2/Rf2 buildup. He has squares, it's true, but few real prospects for initiative.

B2

(1 c4 Nf6 2 g3 g6 3 Bg2 Bg7 4 Nc3 0-0 5 e4 d6 6 Nge2)

6 ...	c5

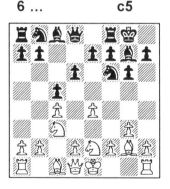

This natural alternative aims to grab a piece of the center without disturbing the Black pawn on *e7*. Then if White advances his f-pawn to the fifth rank, Black will be able to occupy both his *d4* and *e5* with Knights. Note that this could arise out of Section II systems (*1 c4 c5 2 g3 g6*) in which White prefers e4 to e3. In our current move order it arrives by way of 6...c5 after which 7 0-0 Nc6 8 d3 are the natural moves. (By other move orders it can come about, for example, by way of *1 c4 c5 2 g3 Nf6 3 Bg2 g6* and now instead of *4 e3* White can go in for *4 Nc3 Bg7 5 e4 Nc6 6 Nge2 0-0 7 0-0 d6 8 d3*).

7 0-0   Nc6
8 d3

White's plan is no longer f2-f4, but rather d3-d4. (In a pinch he can also shift to a3 and b2-b4). A liquidation in the center with d3-d4 (...cd/N×d4 would work out very well for White.

8 ...   Ne8

Or if 8...a6, then 9 h3 Rb8 (slow Queenside play that is more appropriate to a semi-closed game.) 10 a4 followed by Be3 and d3-d4!.

9 Be3   Nc7

This is consistent but probably inferior to 9...Nd4, preventing White's next move. There is a down side to 9...Nd4 — White has an easier time with b2-b4. After 10 Rb1 Nc7 11 b4 b6 12 Qd2 Bb7 13 f4 f5 14 a4 he has a small edge, e.g., 14...Qd7 15 b×c5 d×c5 16 a5 or 14...Rb8 15 Nb5 Nc×b5 16 a×b5 (Bareev-Gelfand, Munich 1994).

10 d4	c×d4
11 N×d4	Ne6
12 N4e2!	

Avoiding exchanges.

12 ...	Nc5
13 Rc1	Be6
14 b3	Qa5
15 Qd2	

White has a positional advantage due primarily to his greater space (it's a Maroczy bind formation), from the game Barcza-Szilagyim Hungary 1967.

Of course, if Black had tried 8...e5 to stop d3-d4, White continues with his f2-f4 plan because f4-f5 and g4-g5 has become effective again due to the weakness at *f6* and the congestion of Black's pieces.

B3

(1 c4 Nf6 2 g3 g6 3 Bg2 Bg7 4 Nc3 0-0 5 e4 d6 6 Nge2)

6 ...   e5
7 0-0

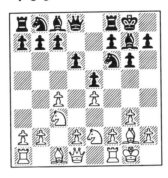

Now play further varies with:

B31 7...Nc6
B32 7...Be6
B33 7...Nfd7
B34 7...Nbd7
B35 7...c5

B31

(1 c4 Nf6 2 g3 g6 3 Bg2 Bg7 4 Nc3 0-0 5 e4 d6 6 Nge2 e5 7 0-0)

7 ...   Nc6

The Knight concentrates on a square White has apparently abandoned, his *d4*. But Black's avoidance of c6 means that his Queen will have no access to the Queenside and, unless White plays d2-d4, his QN and KB will have no particular role in the search for counterplay. White again adopts the f2-f4-f5 plan.

8 f4   Ne8

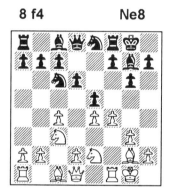

If 8...Bg4 then 9 f5 and 10 h3 is strong while 8...Nd4 9 d3 c5 10 f5! as in Section IA.

If Black captures on *f4* when White plays f2-f4, White recaptures with a pawn and sets up an impregnable wall of center pawns.

B32

(1 c4 Nf6 2 g3 g6 3 Bg2 Bg7 4 Nc3 0-0 5 e4 d6 6 Nge2 e5 7 0-0)

7 ...   Be6

Black tries to exchange off White's fianchettoed Bishop, but since this is a somewhat "bad" Bishop, and since Black's chances of exploiting the Kingside after an exchange of Bishops depends largely on his degree of development, it is not likely to be successful.

8 d3

White has a pleasant choice between this and 8 b3 followed by d4.

8 ...	Qc8
9 f4	Bh3

Or if 9...c6, then 10 f5 g×f5 11 Bg5 (11...N moves, *12 Be7*).

10 f5	B×g2

Of course not 10...g×f5?? 11 B×h3.

11 K×g2

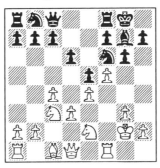

White has excellent chances for a successful Kingside attack.

B33

(1 c4 Nf6 2 g3 g6 3 Bg2 Bg7 4 Nc3 0-0 5 e4 d6 6 Nge2 e5 7 0-0)

| 7 ... | Nfd7 |

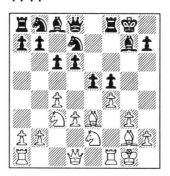

Black concedes his KN is misplaced. A similar idea is 7...Ne8.

8 d3

Also quite good is 8 d4 with a favorable King's Indian proper.

8 ...	c6
9 Be3	f5
10 e×f5	g×f5
11 f4	

White will follow up with 12 f×e5 and 13 d4 with positional advantage. Black doesn't seem to be able to lose this much time (7...Nfd7) when he seeks to open up the position (*9...f5*).

B34

(1 c4 Nf6 2 g3 g6 3 Bg2 Bg7 4 Nc3 0-0 5 e4 d6 6 Nge2 e5 7 0-0)

7 ...	Nbd7
8 d3	

8 ...	c6

With this move Black retains the tactical option of b7-b5 such as after 9 f4?! b5! (*10 c×b5 c×b5 11 N×b5 Qb6ch*). If Black plays routinely with 8...Nc5 he should be run over on the Kingside before he gets anything concrete in the way of counterplay (e.g., *9 f4 c6 10 f5 d5?! 11 f×g6 h×g6 12 e×d5* or *10...b5 11 c×b5 c×b5 12 b4*).

9 h3

Now White can prepare for f4-f5 with 10 Be3. As mentioned earlier, it is insufficient for Black to play 9...Ne8 in response because of constricted positions such as 10 Be3 Qc7 11 f4 f5 12 e×f5 g×f5 13 d4.

9 ...	Nc5

9...a6 will lead back into the note to move six after 10 a4 a5 11 f4.

10 Be3	a5

To avoid b2-b4.

11 f4!	e×f4

12 g×f4!	Qe7
13 Qd2	Rb8

So far as in the game Markland-Hort, Hastings 1970-71, in which a top GM was slaughtered after 14 Rae1 N5d7 15 Ng3 Ne8 16 d4 Nc7 17 e5!.

B35

(1 c4 Nf6 2 g3 g6 3 Bg2 Bg7 4 Nc3 0-0 5 e4 d6 6 Nge2 e5 7 0-0)

7 ...	c5

This seems at first to be a questionable mixture of plans by Black but it has some point. Black wants to occupy *d4* and re-capture with a pawn.

8 h3	Nc6
9 d3	Nd4
10 N×d4	

A good alternative is 10 f4, with 11 f5 in mind.

10 …	e×d4

Here 10…c×d4 has been suggested but Black needs the c-pawn to contain the enemy's queenside initiative (*11 Na4 Nd7 12 b4*).

11 Ne2	Ne8
12 b4!	

And in Skembris-M. Vukic, Krusevac 1994, White had a strong initiative at the cost of a pawn: 12…c×b4 13 a3 b×a3 14 R×a3 Nc7 15 Bb2 and 16 Qa1.

C

(1 c4 Nf6 2 g3)

2 ...	e6
3 Nf3	d5

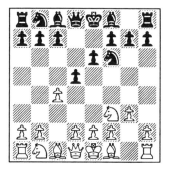

Black's central policy is not as passive as it may seem. He can play c5 at some point, transposing into A of Section II. Or, he can avoid c5 but use a Queenside fianchetto so as to achieve a kind of Queen's Indian Defense in which d4 by White will not force pawn exchanges.

4 b3	Be7

By now we should recognize that 4...c5 is A, of Section II and 4...d4 would transpose into one of the lines considered there after 5 Bb2 c5 6 e3. On the other hand, 4...b6 will reach our main line in this subsection by a different route.

Just about the only piece and pawn configurations that don't transpose into something else are those in which Black puts his KB on *d6*. Here, for example, 4...Bd6 5 Bb2 b6 6 Bg2 Bb7 7 0-0 0-0 is handled most simply by the familiar 8 Nc3 and 9 e3 policy we saw earlier. If Black continues with 8...c5 9 e3 Nc6 he will reach a position from A of Section I in which Black's Bishop is misplaced on *d6* (it blocks the Queen's defense of the d-pawn, for example)

On the other hand 8...a6 (to stop Nb5) 9 e3 Nbd7 10 Qe2 should also be good for White compared to previous examples when the Bishop was on *e7* (*10...e5* is possible here, but *11 Nh4!* is an unpleasant response).

    5 Bg2   **0-0**
    6 0-0

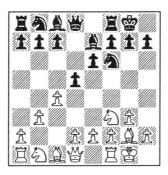

This is where Black must make a pivotal decision. He can't pass much further. we examine:

    C1   6...c6
    C2   6...b6

On 6...Nbd7 Black delays a decision between the two major strategies for one move. In general, he will transpose into one of the lines that follow by move 7 or 8.

C1

(1 c4 Nf6 2 g3 e6 3 Nf3 d5 4 b3 Be7 5 Bg2 0-0 6 0-0)

    6 ...   **c6**

This tends to be too passive unless Black intends b7-b5. It is a solid move that encourages White to set to work in the center with d3 and e4.

7 Bb2	Nbd7
8 d3!	b6

The more active 8...b5 requires a different piece placement by White, Q at *c2* and N at *d2*. Typical play would be 9 Nbd2 Bb7 10 Qc2 a6 11 e4 c5 12 Rfe1 Qb6 13 e5! and 14 d4, or 9...Qb6 10 Qc2 Bb7 11 e4 Rfc8 12 Rfe1 with possibilities of a Kingside attack involving e4-e5 and h2-h4.

C2

(1 c4 Nf6 2 g3 e6 3 Nf3 d5 4 b3 Be7 5 Bg2 0-0 6 0-0)

6 ...	b6

Note that without c7-c6 the QB's diagonal is less obstructed than in (C1).

Interesting is 6...a5, an attempt to take advantage of White's fourth move by way of a4 and even a3. But the move also takes away some of Black's pawn control over *b5* and therefore makes 7 Nc3 a good answer. Black can't play 7...d4 then without allowing the Knight to jump powerfully into *b5*. And if he plays 7...c6 or 7...b6, there doesn't seem to be any point to a5. For instance, 7...c6 8 d4 Nbd7 9 Bb2 and preparations begin for e2-e4.

7 Bb2	Bb7

What is distinctive about this position is Black's avoidance of c5. However, White should still adhere to his buildup of Nc3/e3 and Qe2 — even though he will not be playing d4.

8 e3   Nbd7

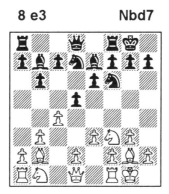

Where else would this Knight go? Now it is available to reach *d3* by way of *c5*. White often plays Qe2 and Nc3 in some order here. For example, 9 Nc3 Ne4 10 c×d5 N×c3 11 B×c3 B×d5 12 Qe2 and now 12...c5 13 Rfd1 Rc8 14 Rac1 Rc7 15 e4 Bb7 16 d4! favors White, as does 13...Qc7 14 Rac1 Qb7 15 d3 Rfd8 16 e4 Bc6 17 Qb2 (Ljubojevic-Belyavsky, Linares 1992).

9 Qe2

Black's minor piece placement may be the most harmonious, but there are still heavy pieces to be developed. This means he will have to play c6 or c5 at some point in order to make luft for his Queen. White's continued strengthening of his position is much easier than Black's.

We now look at two Black replies:

    C21   9...Nc5
    C22   9...a5

C21

(1 c4 Nf6 2 g3 e6 3 Nf3 d5 4 b3 Be7 5 Bg2 0-0 6 0-0 b6 7 Bb2 Bb7 8 e3 Nbd7 9 Qe2)

9 ...   Nc5

This move eyes *d3* but permits White to occupy *d4* with a piece or a pawn.

    10 Nd4   Qd7
    11 Nc3   d×c4

Or if 11...e5, then 12 Nf3 e4 13 Ne5 Qe6 14 Nb5 Rfc8 15 f4 with advantage for White.

    12 B×b7   N×b7
    13 b×c4   c5
    14 Nf3

(see diagram on next page)

White has good chances with a following d4 or Ne5.

Note that 9...dxc4 10 bxc4 Nc5 is no improvement on the line above because Black does not get a chance to occupy *d3* (*11 d4 Nce4 12 Ne5*).

C22

(1 c4 Nf6 2 g3 e6 3 Nf3 d5 4 b3 Be7 5 Bg2 0-0 6 0-0 b6 7 Bb2 Bb7 8 e3 Nbd7 9 Qe2)

9 ...   a5

The immediate 9...Ne4 is immediately pushed back by 10 d3 as 10...Bf6?? loses a piece after 11 dxe4.

10 d3

In the famous game Botvinnik-Stahlberg, Moscow 1956, White played 10 Nc3 after which Black missed 10...a4! with the idea 11 Nxa4 dxc4 12 Qxc4 Ba6.

10 ...   a4

11 Nbd2

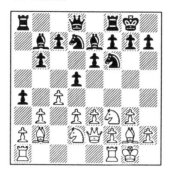

White has promising play by preparing e4-e5.

D

(1 c4 Nf6 2 g3)

2 ...	c6

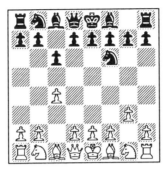

This is a difficult line to crack. The game shifts into a Reti Opening — the way Reti used to play it, that is with c4 rather than e4.

3 b3	d5
4 Bb2	

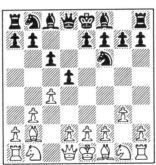

This order of moves avoids surprises such as 4 Bg2 d×c4 5 b×c4 Qd4 or 5 Nf3 c×b3 6 a×b3 e5 (7 *N×e5? Qd4*). Also, on 4 Nf3 Qb6!? White finds that 5 Bb2? d×c4 sets up a pin on the b-file. And 5 Bg2 allows the move White has been trying to avoid — 5...e5! (*6 N×e5? Qd4*). This was the move order of Bent Larsen's disastrous game versus Viktor Korchnoi at S.W.I.F.T. 1987 which continued 6 0-0 e4 7 Ne1 h5! 8 Nc3 h4 9 d4 h×g3 10 f×g3 Qa5 11 Qc2 Bg4! with advantage to Black.

If Black locks in his Bishop with 4...e6 he reaches a position discussed in the note to move 6 of the last subsection. Moreover, Black cannot achieve e7-e5 quickly (*4...Nbd7 5 Nf3 Qc7 6 d4!* and Black's pieces are badly misplaced).

Black has three main alternatives here:

      D1   4...Bg4
      D2   4...g6
      D3   4...Bf5

D1

(1 c4 Nf6 2 g3 c6 3 b3 d5 4 Bb2)

    4 ...   **Bg4**

The chief drawback to 4...Bg4 is that the Bishop doesn't exert enough pressure on Kingside white squares such as *e4*.

    5 Bg2   **Nbd7**
    6 Nf3   **e6**
    7 0-0   **Bd6**

(see diagram on next page)

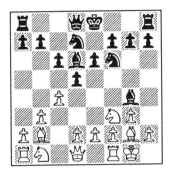

Black aims at ...e5. For this reason it is a mistake to give White a free chance to advance to *d4*, e.g., 7...a5 8 a3 Bc5? 9 d4! Bd6 10 Nbd2 followed by preparations for e2-e4 or 9...Bb6 10 Nbd2 0-0 (Markowski-Lalic, Biel 1995) and now 11 b4!.

8 d4!   0-0

Or 8...Qb8 9 Nbd2 0-0 10 Re1 Re8 11 e4 with a slight plus in the center.

9 Nc3	**Qe7**
10 Qc1	**Rac8**
11 Re1	**c5**
12 c×d5	**B×f3**

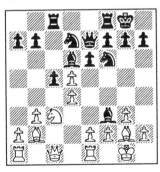

On 12...N×d5 White has 13 Ne4.

13 d×c5	**N×c5**
14 B×f3	

As in Korchnoi-Lutikov, Kiev 1965 White has a big advantage.

D2

(1 c4 Nf6 2 g3 c6 3 b3 d5 4 Bb2)

4 ...	g6

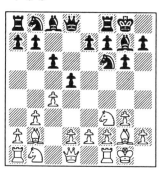

In our discussion of the King's Indian Defense (B) we saw White piled up on his *d5*. This position is different because White has little immediate firepower trained on *d5*.

5 Nf3

The natural reaction.

5 ...	Bg7
6 Bg2	0-0
7 0-0	

One of Black's problems here is what to do with his QB — it will get into trouble on *f5*.

7 ...	Bg4

On 7...a5 8 c×d5 c×d5 9 Nc3 Nc6 10 d4 and Ne5. Or 7...Nbd7 8 c×d5 c×d5 9 Nc3 e5 10 d4 e4 11 Ne5.

8 h3

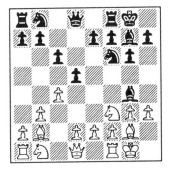

White's position is better. White can also delay this in favor of 8 d3 Nbd7 9 Nbd2 so that he can retake on *f3* with a knight. Then 9...Re8 10 h3 B×f3 11 N×f3 e5 again leaves White with a slight edge. If he doesn't want to allow ...e6-e5, White can try 10 d4, e.g., 10...Qb6 11 Ne5 N×e5 12 d×e5 Nd7 13 c×d5 c×d5 14 B×d5 N×e5 15 B×e5 B×e5 16 Nc4 (Hodgson-Gelfand, Biel 1995).

D3

(1 c4 Nf6 2 g3 c6 3 b3 d5 4 Bb2)

4 ...   Bf5

5 Bg2	e6
6 Nf3	Nbd7

Black can also delay the development of the QN in order to see if Na6 will work out better. For example, 6...h6 7 0-0 Be7 8 d3 0-0 and 9...Bh7. But the Knight on *a6* is most likely to go to *c5* when possible — and in our main line must be available for Black to go to *b6* in an emergency.

7 0-0   h6

This cannot be delayed indefinitely because Black needs an escape square for his Bishop after an eventual Nh4. White has delayed that diversion so far because he is not developed enough to afford it. But later...

8 d3   Be7

A degree of timing is required: 8...Bh7 is questionable because White has time to act in the center: 9 Nbd2 and if 9...Bc5, then 10 e4 d×e4 11 d×e4 Qe7 (capturing on *e4* lets White capture later on *g7*) 12 Qe2 e5 13 a3 0-0 14 b4 Bb6 15 Ne1 a5 16 Nd3 followed by c5 and Nc4 with advantage, as in the game Fuderer-Cortlever, Amsterdam, 1954.

9 Nbd2   0-0
10 a3   a5

Black cannot allow White to expand on the Queenside with b2-b4 uncontested.

11 Qc2   Bh7

Originally, when this variation became popular for Black, it was thought that he could exert pressure on the weakened Queenside with Qb6. But recent discoveries have shown that

Black needs b7-b5 instead. After 11...Qb6 White gets a good game with the maneuver Bc3 and Qb2, e.g., 12 Bc3 Rfd8 13 Qb2 Nc5 14 Bd4 d×c4 15 d×c4 Qc7 16 b4!.

12 Rfb1!

This prepares Bc3/Qb2. The older version of this was the immediate 12 Bc3 and now 12...b5 13 c×b5 c×b5 14 Qb2 Qb6 15 b4 a×b4 16 a×b4 gives White a slight edge because of his strength on the a1/g7 diagonal and on the queenside (Nb3-a5). For example, 16...Rfc8 17 R×a8 R×a8 18 Nb3 Bd6 19 Ra1! R×a1 20 Q×a1 with a superior endgame, thanks to control of the open file, or 19...Re8 20 Bd4 Qb8 21 Bc5! e5 22 Ra6! and White is creeping up (Ribli-Sherzer, Hungary 1995).

This new move appears to give White a continuing initiative. Black is restrained from opening the c-file (12...b5 13 Nd4, Qb6 14 c×d5 c×d5 15 Qc6!) and needs some preparation. The recommended line is:

12 ...   Qb8

But now White's Bc3 maneuver is again strong.

13 Bc3	b5
14 c×d5	c×d5
15 b4	a×b4
16 B×b4!	B×b4
17 a×b4	

(see diagram on next page)

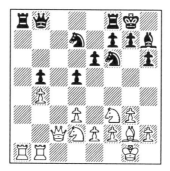

Now 17...Nb6 runs into 18 Ra5!* , and 17...Qb6 permits 18 R×a8 and Nb3-a5. Best is 17...Qd6, but White is still better with 18 Qb3 according to West German GM Robert Huebner.

---

* 18...Nc4! appears to equalize for Black - Ed.

SECTION IV
OTHER SYSTEMS OF DEFENSE

Since most everything solid or well-coordinated will transpose at some point into one of the variations considered on previous pages, this section serves mainly to mop up transpositions and cite the few independent lines worth looking at.

They include:

A   1...e6
B   1...c6
C   1...f5
D   1...b6
E   1...d6 and 1...g6

There is not much to be said about 1...d5 which loses time after 2 c×d5 Q×d5 3 Nc3 Qa5 4 d4 Nf6 5 Nf3 or unsoundly risks material after 2...Nf6 3 e4 c6 (Not *3...N×e4?? 4 Qa4ch*) 4 d×c6 N×c6 5 Nc3 e5 6 Nf3 followed by Bc4 and d3.

A

1 c4	e6
2 Nf3	

Now 2...c5 transposes into (A) of Section II; 2...f5 will transpose into (C) of this Section; 2...b6 will reach (D) of this Section; 2...Nf6 will create (C) of Section III and that leaves only ...

2 ...	d5
3 b3	

And here 3...c5, 3...d4, and 3...Nf6 will also transpose into previously explored territory. Attempts to find something completely new turn out badly (e.g., *3...Qf6 4 Nc3*; *3...Be7 4 Bb2 Bf6 5 d4 Ne7 6 Nbd2* and *7 e4*, etc.). Solider is 3...c6 4 g3 f5, heading into the Dutch formation that we examine in greater detail in (C) below. Black's early commitment to the "Stonewall" pawn formation, characterized by pawns at *c6*, *d5*, *e6* and *f5*, gives White some extra options. For example, 5

Bg2 Nf6 6 0-0 Be7 and now 7 Ba3, to exchange off the dark-squared bishops and be in a better position to exploit holes such as *e5*.

An example of this was Vladimirov-Moskalenko, Helsinki 1992, in which Black tries to repair the main hole with 7...B×a3 8 N×a3 e5 — a trap based on 9 N×e5? Qe7, forking the two knights.   But 9 c×d5 gave White a clear positional edge (*9...c×d5? 10 N×e5 Qe7 11 Qc1!* or *9...Q×d5 10 d3* or *9...e4 10 Nd4 c×d5 11 Rc1 0-0 12 Nab5*).

B

1 c4   c6

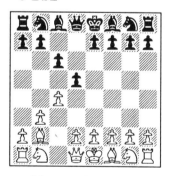

This may be adopted by players who don't like 1...Nf6 2 Nc3 c6 because of 3 e4 d5 4 e5 or 4 c×d5 c×d5 5 e5. Of course, we wouldn't play 2 Nc3. But he doesn't know that.

2 b3   d5

Black may seek a King's Indian-like setup with 2...d6 3 Bb2 e5 4 g3 Nf6, but 5 d4 (or 4 e3 and 5 d4) is much more aggressive and takes advantage of Black's quiet play in the center. For example, 5 d4 e×d4 6 Q×d4 d5 7 Nc3 gives White some pressure in the center.

3 Bb2

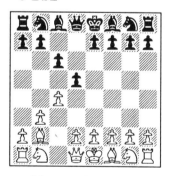

Now to avoid transposition to D of Section III, we would have to try something like 3...Qb6 (which threatens *4...d×c4* but can be handled easily by *4 e3* and *Nc3*). Also, 3...d×c4 4 b×c4 Qb6 is met by 5 Qb3 since the endgame is excellent for White.

C

1 c4   f5

This, at least, is a truly independent line — the Dutch Defense.

There is a temptation here to turn the opening book back into a normal Dutch with 2 d4, since the Dutch is hardly the terror of the Closed Game world. But we'll keep the White opening strategy in character with a particularly English-like approach to 1...f5.

2 g3

Note that this discourages 2...b6 because of 3 Bg2. If Black wants to fianchetto his QB in a Dutch-like setup, he should try to get it by way of 1 c4 b6.

2 ...   Nf6

2...e5 brings us way back to a position considered in C of Section I. Black has other pawn moves, such as 2...g6, 2...d6 or 2...e6, but they are not as flexible as 2...Nf6 and we'll consider them at a later point. Unless Black is going to bring his KN out to h6, as Michael Basman has tried in England, we can assume that Nf6 will be played. This is why 2...Nf6 is the natural order of things.

As for 2...Nh6 or 2...g6 followed by Bg7 and Nh6, this has the drawback of encouraging an early h4-h5. For example, 2...Nh6 3 Bg2 g6 4 h4! Bg7 5 h5. White can open the h-file at will, but won't do it until he has placed his KN at *f4* so that *g6* is under attack. White can also use the possibility of e4 as a weapon because Black puts no pressure on his *e4* square when he plays "a la Basman". For instance, 2...g6 3 Bg2 Bg7 4 Nc3 Nh6 5 h4 Nf7 6 e4! followed by h5. Black's *g6* square comes in for a pounding.

3 Bg2   e6

The Leningrad system, with 3...g6, can be a dangerous alternative. The simplest way of handling the variation is to let Black achieve e7-e5 and then play the position as if it had arisen out of a sequence from Section I. That is, White will play something like 4 Nc3 Bg7 5 d4 d6 6 e3 0-0 7 Nge2 followed by 8 b3 and 9 Bb2. Black will eventually have to play either c6 or Nc6, thereby returning the position to Section I.

4 Nf3

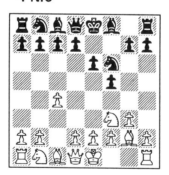

There is no reason to rush into Nc3, which may run into d5-d4, unless White is primed for an early e4. The reason we recommend 4 Nf3 instead is that it permits White to postpone the question of his play in the center (d3 or d4?) for a few more moves.

4 ...   Be7

Also note that 4 Nc3 might encourage 4...Bb4, whereas there is no point to 4...Bb4? here.

But Black can decide to put his Bishop on d6 if he plays d5 first. One order of moves that permits this is 4...d5 5 0-0 Bd6 when White should control his *d4* and *e5* with a fianchettoed QB: 6 b3 0-0 7 Bb2 c6 8 d3. Black cannot occupy his e4 with his pieces now because of the White d-pawn. That d-pawn also enables White to open lines with e4 after it has been prepared with Nbd2 and Qc2. For example, 8...Nbd7 9 Nbd2 Qe7 10 Qc2 f4?! 11 d4! f×g3 12 h×g3 Ng4 13 e4!, Polugaevsky-Durao, Lugano 1968.

5 0-0   0-0
6 d3!

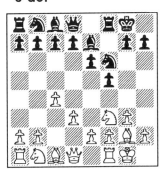

White could delay a choice between d3 and d4 even further (i.e., with 6 b3). But if he decides in favor of d3 at some later point, it will be hard for him to get a Queenside initiative going with Rb1 and b2-b4 with a Bishop in the way on the b-file.

Now Black can choose between two d-pawn moves:
<blockquote>
C1   6...d5
C2   6...d6
</blockquote>

C1

(1 c4 f5 2 g3 Nf6 3 Bg2 e6 4 Nf3 Be7 5 0-0 0-0 6 d3)

6 ...   d5

Black always has a choice in the Dutch-like position between a flexible center (...d6) and a Stonewall center (...d5).

7 b3

White's piece placement will include a Bishop on *b2*, a Knight on *d2*, and his Queen probably at *c2*. This enables him to control his *d4* and *e5* with pieces and his *e4* with the d-pawn as well as QN. Since Black has blocked the *d5* square with his wall of pawns, there is no reason to advance his d-pawn further ...unless. The "unless" comes alive if Black should ever take White's opening strategy for passivity and play c5, a move that greatly loosens the Stonewall.

7 ...   c6

Black has others:

C11 7...c5?
C12 7...Bd7

C11

(1 c4 f5 2 g3 Nf6 3 Bg2 e6 4 Nf3 Be7 5 0-0 0-0 6 d3 d5 7 b3)

7 ...	c5

As mentioned, c7-c5 from a Stonewall is usually too loosening,

8 c×d5	e×d5
9 Bb2	Nc6
10 d4!	

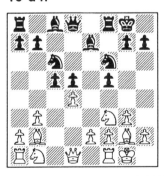

White's advantage is clear — on 10...b6?! 11 d×c5 b×c5 12 Nc3 and the center is under heavy fire, as in Pirc-Tolush, Yugoslavia-USSR Match 1957.

C12

(1 c4 f5 2 g3 Nf6 3 Bg2 e6 4 Nf3 Be7 5 0-0 0-0 6 d3 d5 7 b3)

7 ...   c6

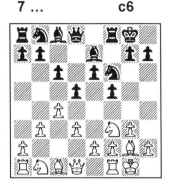

An interesting alternative is 7...Bd7, hoping to activate his "bad" QB via *e8* and *g6* or *h5*. From the diagram, the game Smyslov-Spassky, Candidates Tournament 1956, continued 8 Bb2 Be8 9 Nbd2 Nc6 (or *9...c6 10 Qc2 a5 11 Rae1* and *e4*) 10 a3! a5 11 Qc2 Qd7 12 c×d5 e×d5 13 e3! Bh5 14 Bc3 and White can follow up with Qb2 and Nd4 with a positional advantage.

8 Bb2   Qe8

If Black plays passively, White will choose a white-square strategy involving e4. For example, 8...b6 9 Qc2 Bb7 10 Nbd2 Na6 11 a3 c5?! 12 Rfe1 and ultimately e4, from Milic-Smederevac, Yugoslav Championship 1955. 8...Nbd7 will likely transpose into the main line.

9 Nbd2   Nbd7

(see diagram on next page)

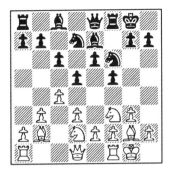

Also possible is 9...Qh5, although it is not particularly danger-ous because of 10 Ne5 and Ndf3, a regrouping maneuver common to Stonewall formations.

10 Qc2

We can see the shape of things to come and they all spell e4 for White. This thrust will have more immediate impact than anything Black can scare up on the Kingside.

| 10 ... | Qh5 |
| 11 e4 | |

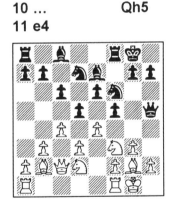

Watson suggests 11 Rae1 first.

11 ...	d×e4
12 d×e4	f4
13 g×f4	Ng4

Threatening 14...R×f4 and a possible sacrifice on f3.

14 h3   Nh6

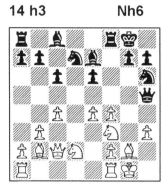

And now 15 Ng5! assures White a clear superiority in the center and a safe Kingside (Filip-Guimard, Goteborg 1955). Suggested improvements include 13...Qh6, but 14 Be5 should keep White on top. White has the d-file for the taking, but Black is playing with only a few pieces.

C2

(1 c4 f5 2 g3 Nf6 3 Bg2 e6 4 Nf3 Be7 5 0-0 0-0 6 d3)

6 ...   d6

This is a more flexible attempt, guarding the vital e5 square.

7 Nc3   e5
8 Rb1

White intends to advance the b-pawn.

8 ...   c6

If 8...a5, to slow up b2-b4, then 9 a3 Qe8 10 b4 a×b4 11 a×b4 Nc6 12 b5 Nd8 13 c5! is strong. If Black plays 13...d×c5 he loses his more valuable e-pawn. Also, the series of exchanges of pawns that are inevitable in the early middle game are bound to favor White (*13...Ne6 14 cd cd 15 b6!* - threatening Nb5 - *15...Bd7 16 Ng5! N×g5 17 B×g5*).

9 b4	Kh8
10 b5	

Favorably opening Queenside lines.

10 ...	Qc7
11 Qa4	a6
12 b×c6	N×c6
13 Bd2	Bd7
14 Rfc1	

Intending Nd5. White's advantage is clear, Ree-Farago, Students Olympiade 1966.

D

1 c4   b6

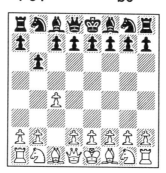

At last a move that stops 2 g3 and 3 Bg2.

2 Nf3

There are other moves, but to be consistent, we must consider this position because it might arise after 1 c4 e6 2 Nf3 b6.

2 ...   Bb7
3 g3

The counter fianchetto is the simplest policy. Inevitably there will be either an exchange of Bishops or the advance of a pawn — White or Black — to the square White calls *d5*. This will restrict Black's pieces or weaken his white-colored squares. Note that White defers an advance of his d-pawn or QN until ...Bb4 is no longer feasible.

3 ...   e6

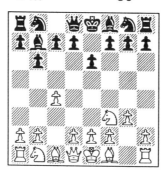

Also of interest is 3...B×f3?!, a violent alternative, hoping to undermine White's Kingside squares and hem in his Bishop. But the hemming-in is brief and f4 (and f5) are in the future. After 4 e×f3:

(1)   4...e6 5 f4 d5 6 Bg2 Nf6 7 0-0 and now Black must be wary of f5 (*7...Nbd7 8 f5; 7...Be7 8 f5 e×f5 9 Nc3 c6 10 c×d5 c×d5 11 Qb3*).

(2)   4...c5 5 d4 c×d4 6 Q×d4 Nc6 7 Qd2 and White will fianchetto both Bishops with an excellent game.

Also, 3...f5 is an idea, as is 3...Nf6, e.g., 3...Nf6 4 Bg2 e5 using the pin on the long diagonal. White would then castle and wait for Black to cover his central squares (*5 0-0 d6 6 Nc3 and 7 d3/8 e4/9 Nh4 and 10 f4 or 5...e4 6 Nd4 d5?! 7 c×d5 Q×d5 8 Qa4ch*).

4 Bg2   Nf6

The problem with 4...f5 is the continued weakness on certain central squares that leaves Black susceptible to d4-d5. White won't want the d-pawn advanced until Bb4ch is out of the picture, but eventually the pawn will march, e.g., 4...f5 5 0-0 Nf6 6 d4 and with the following main possibilities:

6...Be7 7 d5! e×d5 8 Nd4 g6 9 Nc3

6...c5 7 d5 e×d5 8 Nh4 g6 9 Nc3 Be7 10 N×d5

6...Qc8 7 Bg5 Be7 8 d5.

5 0-0

Now, either 5...Be7 6 b3, 5...d5 6 b3, or 5...c5 6 b3 returns us to positions considered in Sections II and III.

E

1 c4   d6

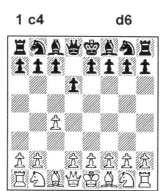

With this move Black indicates he intends to fianchetto his KB, but isn't about to advertise that fact. The advertisement would have been 1...g6 which leads to more familiar ground by way of 2 g3 c5; 2...Bg7 3 Bg2 e5 or 3...f5, or just 3...Nf6 - a transposition into each of the previous Sections.

2 g3

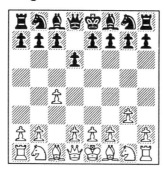

Here 2...e5 is C of Section I, while 2...f5 is likely to reach that line in a few moves. 2...Nf6 most likely will enter the King's Indian Defense of Section III, and 2...c5 will find its way into one of the pages of our second Section.

One thing that may make Black's formation unique is where he puts his knights. For example, 1...g6 2 g3 Bg7 3 Bg2 e5 4 Nc3 d6 5 d3 and now 5...Nd7 6 e4 Ne7 is an unusual placement of the knights on *e7* and *d7* for a possible shift in either direction (...Nf6 followed by ...c6 and ...d5 is one option.)

(Analysis diagram following 6...Ne7)

Play might continue 7 Nge2 0-0 8 Be3 f5 9 Qd2 Nf6 10 Bg5!
c6 11 0-0 Be6 12 Rae1 so that White can meet 12...d5 with
13 exd5 cxd5 14 Nf4!. In Pavlovic-Grivas, Karditsa 1994,
White obtained a useful advantage after 12...Qd7 13 b3 d5 14
f4!, e.g., 14...dxe4 15 fxe5 exd3 16 exf6 dxe2 17 Qxe2 Bxf6
18 Bxf6 and 19 Qe5 or 14...dxc4 15 fxe5 cxd3! 16 exf6 dxe2
17 Qxd7.

CONCLUSION:

As long as White keeps aware of the possibilities of surprise
transpositions — which he can usually do with an early g3/Bg2
followed by castling and then a Queenside fianchetto — he
will keep control of the position and, perhaps more importantly,
keep control of the openings he wants to play.

Happy Middlegames! - This new revised edition confirms the
strengths of the 2 g3 lines of the English Opening.

NOTES

NOTES

NOTES